In *The Productive Researcher,* Mark Reed shows researchers how they can become more productive in a fraction of their current working day. He draws on interviews with some of the world's highest performing researchers, the literature and his own experience to identify a small number of important insights that can transform how researchers work. The book is based on an unparalleled breadth of interdisciplinary evidence that speaks directly to researchers of all disciplines and career stages. The lessons in this book will make you more productive, more satisfied with what you produce, and enable you to be happy working less, and being more.

Mark Reed is Professor of Socio-Technical Innovation at Newcastle University and Visiting Professor at Birmingham City University and the University of Leeds. He has over 150 publications that have been cited more than 15,000 times. He is author of *The Research Impact Handbook,* which he has used to train over 8000 researchers from more than 200 institutions in 55 countries.

THE
PRODUCTIVE
RESEARCHER

Mark S. Reed

Fast Track Impact

Second edition published 2019
First published 2017
by Fast Track Impact www.fasttrackimpact.com
St Johns Well, Kinnoir, Huntly, Aberdeenshire AB54 7XT

British Library Cataloguing-in-Publication Data
A catalogue record for this book is available from the British
Library

This book should be cited as:
Reed, M.S. (2019). The Productive Researcher. 2nd Edition, Fast
Track Impact.

ISBN: 978-0-9935482-2-2 (pbk)
ISBN: 978-0-9935482-3-9 (ebk)

Design by: Anna Sutherland
Photography by: Joyce Reed

To Hanifa, for your calm belief in wild possibilities

Contents

1 Introduction   1

Part 1: Principles
2 Smart-grid your motivation   13
3 Retell your story   29
4 Single-mindedly prioritise   47
5 Find goals that inspire you: the new SMART   57

Part 2: Making it happen
6 Plans that work   73
7 Say "yes" to say "no"   89
8 How to write a literature review in a week   103
9 Do less to do more   117
10 How to spend less time on emails and
     meetings   135
11 How to spend less time online   145

12 Conclusion   155
Acknowledgements   160
Appendix 1: Ten of the most productive
                researchers in the world   162
Appendix 2: Power questionnaire   164
Endnotes   166

Chapter 1

The one thing we want as researchers is time; time to write up our latest work, and time to feel like we have a life. Surely, that's not asking too much?

Fortunately for me, it appears that time is on my side. Something strange seems to happen to time when I work, and until recently, I was unable to explain it.

It was genuinely baffling. Journal articles, books and projects just seemed to happen. I had this really weird recurring argument with my most prolific co-author: "you have to be first author on this one", I told her, "because I hardly wrote any of it". She would reply that I had to be first author because she felt like she had hardly written anything either. I had a full teaching allocation in every position I held (based on workload models) until I took my current position, eighteen months ago. Yet, I have had time to run an international spin-out company (Fast Track Impact), work as Research Lead for a conservation charity, run a podcast, blog and magazine, manage six Twitter accounts and advise the United Nations and governments around the world, based on my research. Over the last 3 years since joining Newcastle University, I published 29 peer-reviewed articles (5 as lead author) and 3 books, and been awarded 13 new research projects (5 as Principal Investigator) worth over £2M to my institution. I have done this whilst being Director of Engagement and Impact for my school for half of this time, sitting on various university committees and working groups, and training more than 5000 researchers.

This has all happened without working weekends, or working beyond my contracted hours.

Maybe this is a British thing, but over the years this became increasingly embarrassing for me. There were three reasons for this. First, researchers who didn't know how much I worked assumed that there must be something wrong with me; I must be a workaholic or on some kind of "spectrum". I could see them pitying my wife and family, and feeling grateful that they had more "normal" lives.

The second problem was that when I attempted to explain to these colleagues how much I actually worked, they didn't believe me. I have had a message at the bottom of my emails for some time saying, "I work two evenings a week, so if this email arrives outside office hours, please do not feel you have to reply until normal working hours". My colleagues suggested that if I worked five days a week including two evenings, then I must be underestimating my working hours. I thought they had a point, so I downloaded a time-tracker app and logged every minute of work I did for five representative weeks. To my astonishment, when I did the calculation to work out my hours per week, the answer was 37 (of all numbers). When I drilled into the data, I discovered that on Mondays and Fridays when I work from home, I work surprisingly little (often just four hours). Still, colleagues objected; arguing that the levels of productivity and success I was experiencing would not have been possible without someone at home looking after my children and household. However, until I moved to Newcastle University in 2016, my wife worked away from home three nights a week doing a 36-hour week as a hospital doctor and, with limited childcare options, when she was working I had to be at home to put children to school and bed, and all the other things a parent needs to do to run a house in the absence of their partner. As a result, I had to say "no" to multiple opportunities that would have created childcare issues for us as a family.

The third problem was that those who eventually believed me, or who already knew how much I worked, kept asking me to mentor them. They would come to me with great anticipation, only to discover that I had no idea how I did what I did.

In an attempt to work out what was going on, I began reaching out to colleagues with similar experiences. Talking to them, I began to realise that we were doing a number of similar things. To test the theory that was beginning to form in my mind, I did what any self-respecting researcher would do: I started reading. I read broadly, forming hypotheses that could link ideas from very different disciplines. I also reached out to some of the world's most productive researchers (Appendix 1), based on their publications and citations, according to *Times Higher Education*'s use of Elsevier's SciVal tool, and asked them how they did what they do. Their answers and the answers that emerged from my reading both confirmed and extended my thinking. In this book, I want to share with you what I learned.

My goal is not to squeeze more productivity out of already over-worked researchers. Most of us feel performance-managed and measured to within an inch of our lives, by ever more demanding employers, who operate increasingly like businesses. Where did the time go, to just think? I don't want to work any harder than I already do; I want to work easier. I want to be more productive so I can get my thinking time back, and have more free time.

If you are serious about becoming more productive, you need to become serious about taking time off – properly. Become more productive to spend less time working. Spend less time working to become more productive.

A lesson from a man with very white teeth

As an interdisciplinary researcher, I looked for evidence from a wide range of disciplines to test the insights I gleaned from the researchers I interviewed and my own experience. As a result, many of the insights in this book are quite different to those that are often repeated by the business and economics authors who tend to write books about productivity.

As I extended my reading to this popular genre, I found much that was helpful and much that made me cringe. At first, I thought I was just being an academic snob: "stop telling me you're going to change my life and show me your sources", I felt like yelling at many a page. However, as I pushed through my snobbery, I realise that I was cringing at a set of assumptions that was implicit in much of the genre. (Okay, I have to admit that some of these books were not so "implicit" about getting rich overnight and using your newfound riches to become an experience junkie and travel the world.)

Whether explicit or implicit, the one thing that these books all seemed to assume was that we all want to optimise every part of our lives: our minds; our bodies; our relationships; without ever asking why. Why do we need to change ourselves? Why do we need to be healthier and more liked? Where do these messages come from, and who is profiting from telling us the answers? For me personally, the answers to these questions were revealing. I've never wanted more money than I needed to give my family a safe and nurturing environment. I am no longer trying to gain the approval of my peers. I don't have any expectation of long life (I come from a line of men who have died of heart attacks in their forties).

Then, I actually met one of the authors who had made his fortune from the productivity industry. In a "meta" twist, he had written a self-help book aimed at people who wanted to get rich by writing self-help books. With a dazzling white smile, he explained that there was a reason why he wrote "best-selling" not "best-written" books. He went on to reveal his secret formula: speak your book into your phone, get it transcribed online, launch it in an obscure category on the Kindle store where nothing is selling, get "best-seller" status in that category, and then market yourself as a "best-selling author" to earn speaker fees.

The irony, you will tell me, is that here I am, writing a book to help researchers become more productive. The irony is not lost on me. However, despite being shocked by what I found at the core of the productivity industry, it helped me articulate how I do what I do. I realise that it had very little to do with productivity techniques; I could try all the techniques that had ever been devised and get no further forward, if I lacked clarity of thinking.

The problem with techniques

The problem with techniques is that there are so many of them, and no single technique will work for everyone. Most researchers already have multiple time-management and productivity techniques to choose from, and have already worked out what works for them. I want to provide practical help, but I don't want this to be a book of techniques. Instead, I want to show you how you can think differently. I want to challenge your thinking, so you can discover the power of the techniques you already know.

Most of the people who tell me they have a problem with time management don't actually have a problem with time management. Most people who say their teaching and administration is getting in the way of their research don't actually have any more teaching and administration than the most productive researchers had at the same point in their career. It is often easier to externalise our problems than it is to address their root causes.

There are many causes of procrastination and low productivity, but one I find hiding at the root of many researchers' frustrations is a fundamental lack of confidence. It is the ghost of the reviewer telling them everything that's wrong as they write, or the belief that what they produce must be perfect or they will be judged, found wanting and not given a second chance.

The solution is not to look for a new writing technique or time-management system, but to try and tackle the source of your fear. Often, this fear is deeply buried under a career of expert pronouncements and international accolades that you have gathered around yourself to protect you from that nagging inner voice of doubt. Some researchers just find it difficult to focus; a lack of clear, value-driven motivation can make distractions more attractive than the task in hand. The solution is not to look for a new, more interesting job or project, but to tap into a deeper motivation that empowers you to get the job done faster and more effectively.

In this book, I want to help you find ways to achieve your research aspirations without becoming a workaholic. To do this, you may have to face issues that are rooted deeply in your experiences so far as a researcher. The longer you hide from these issues, the more you are likely to fall short of your aspirations. You can blame others or you can blame yourself. Either way, the danger is that you feed into a negative narrative that further disempowers you.

I speak from experience. I grew up with a chronic lack of self-confidence due to abuse I suffered as a child. This fed directly into my early career as a researcher. I had a panic attack in the middle of my first lecture in front of over 200 students (one of whom started heckling me). The first paper I submitted as an academic was rejected with a one-liner from the editor saying, "this reads like a bad term paper". My first grant application was slammed as "pedestrian science". I crashed and burned at one of the biggest opportunities of my early career in front of a packed hall of researchers, policymakers and research funders when I panicked and went completely blank during the panel debate. The Chair, Sir Howard Newby, then head of the Higher Education Funding Council for England prompted "I think this one's for you Mark", and to my excruciating embarrassment, all I could say was "I know". Not long after that, I crashed and burned in front of the entire world (literally), when I failed to prepare for the fact that my talk on deliberative democracy might provoke a hostile political reaction from the Chinese policymakers attending the 9th Conference of the Parties to the UN Convention to Combat Desertification.

On bad days, experiences like these fed into a negative story I told about myself. However, I was fortunate that there was a deeper narrative I was always able to tap into. I first heard that story from my grandmother, who told me about my great grandparents and their parents who had been some of the first missionaries in central Africa. She told me about the suffering they had borne and the challenges they had overcome for the sake of their convictions. The subconscious narrative I learned as a young boy, listening to her stories, was that it was inevitable that I would do something on a similar scale. As a child, I didn't ask how. I just believed that I too must be capable of something great. As an adult, I drew on this belief and started building my own counter-narrative to the story of shame I frequently found myself mired in. If, as a result of my research, I could do something to make the world a better place, then I felt like I was somehow counteracting the bad things that had happened to me when I was growing up. I had found a deeper purpose, which I then harnessed to drive my research.

How to do more and better research, and get your life back

So how do I get more done while achieving a work-life balance? In a nutshell, I focus on my most important priorities and pursue them consistently every week. I am creating a positive feedback loop between my priorities and my motivation. By focusing on my priorities, I feel more motivated. Because I'm more motivated, I focus more on my priorities. Creating this positive feedback loop is easy. Focus on doing something that is deeply important to you for ten minutes a day, or 30 minutes once a week, and you'll discover a new sense of progress and purpose that enables you to keep investing time in your priorities consistently. I am not advocating selfishly pursuing your goals at the expense of your team, but if you are unable to devote just 30 minutes a week to something that is important to you, then you need to take a long, hard look at what's driving your decisions.

In this book, I will show you how you can create this powerful feedback loop, so you find new sources of motivation that inspire you to make consistent progress towards your priorities. I will do this by sharing a number of generalisable principles that emerged from my reading and interviews in part 1. Then in part 2, I will show you how you can apply these principles in practice. Although I have written this book specifically for researchers, as I've discussed the book with friends outside academia, I have found that many of the key messages resonate more widely. However, if you are reading this and you are not a researcher, you may want to skip over a few of the contextual details. I have written the book from my position as a University Professor, but I am mindful of the very different challenges I faced 12 years ago as a PhD student. Whether you are an early career researcher or more experienced, the principles in part 1 of this book should be both relevant and powerful. Although some of the advice in part 2 appears more relevant to experienced researchers, learning how to say "no" and manage distractions early, may prevent you from losing the motivation and focus you currently enjoy.

The principles in first part of the book are derived from the literature, interviews with researchers and my own experience. They are more than just theory. They have emerged from lived experience and are designed to be lived. I will show you ways to (re-)discover clear and empowering motives and (re-)write your internal narrative, so that you achieve a kind of productivity that isn't about meeting targets or keeping your employer and peers happy. It may not be about writing books, papers or grants, or climbing the career ladder; it may not even be about your research. I want to focus on a kind of productivity that gives you a sense of satisfaction on a fundamental level, and that is as much about who you are outside work, as much as it is about who you are as a researcher.

The researchers I interviewed knew exactly why they were doing what they were doing, every minute of every day. Your reasons, like theirs, don't need to be profound or complicated. They just need to connect to who you are as a person. Some of us are doing this so we can give our children the childhood we dreamt of having. Some of us are doing this to find a place of creative solitude where we might eventually find peace, or some deeper meaning. Some of us are fuelled by an insatiable curiosity to understand the world around us, or our place in it, and we become more enthralled the deeper we delve.

Part 2 of this book focuses on practical methods for applying the principles outlined in the first part. While the aim of these chapters is to provide practical guidance, the focus remains on changing how you think, and illustrating how each of the principles in the first part of the book may be put into practice. Throughout the book, I've developed exercises you can use to apply what you've learned. I have developed most of these over a number of years and have used them in mentoring, coaching and training sessions with colleagues who have found them transformative.

I have illustrated the book with stories from my own experience to show the real-life applicability of the principles outlined in part 1. In doing so, I don't intend to hold myself up us an example to follow. Rather, I hope to show that I am just as fallible, error-prone and human as every other researcher. Each of us has many barriers to overcome if we are to reach our goals. I hope that by sharing part of my personal story, I may spur others to find new ways of overcoming the unique barriers that face them. I hope that by integrating insights from my own experience with lessons from the literature and from those I interviewed for this book, I have developed principles that are sufficiently broad and deep to apply in your own unique circumstances.

Why now?

I believe that researchers need these ideas now more than ever. More and more PhDs are being awarded, but the rate of funding and jobs isn't keeping pace, which is driving increased and intense competition. Finding ways to become more productive may help early career researchers secure a long-term academic role, and start their careers the way they intend to continue, protecting their work-life balance.

For those who have secured such a role, the pressures are different but no less intense. More than a third of UK academics responding to a 2012 survey said that they worked more than 50 hours per week[i]. Two years later, that figure had risen to 41%[ii], and by 2016, academics were working 51 hours per week on average[iii]. Figures are similar in the United States, with postdocs working 51 hours per week[iv] and faculty staff working 55 hours per week[v].

For most of us, those hours would be fine if we felt we were actually achieving what we wanted. Sadly, most of us are familiar with the feeling of leaving work with a to-do list that is longer than when we started the day. As a result, most researchers I know regularly work on many evenings and weekends. This is often the only time they can find to do some of the most important parts of their job, like writing, after their working day has been eaten up by endless administrative tasks, teaching and emails. An ex-colleague of mine recently told me how he had taken a 40% pay cut by going part-time so he could get his evenings and weekends back (he now works 40 hours a week).

It doesn't have to be like this. It is possible to do more and better research *and* get your life back. It took me half my career to work it out, but I now know how I and many other researchers have done it. This book explains how you can do it too.

Part 1: **Principles**

Chapter 2
Smart-grid your motivation

Motivated researchers are productive researchers. Motivation generates productivity for three reasons: it gives you drive, focus and staying power.

If you want to be more productive, you need to find ways to fuel your sense of drive. You need drive to start your Monday morning with enthusiasm and anticipation for the week ahead. Part of you may want to continue reading the news or browsing social media a bit longer, but your sense of excitement and purpose makes it easy to turn on your computer and start your day. You need drive to make the conscious decision to continue writing when the people next to you on your flight or train have fallen asleep. You need drive to dream big, believe you can achieve your dreams, and say "yes" when an opportunity arises to fulfil your dream before you feel ready. **Having powerful motives fuels your drive.**

If you want to be more productive, you need to find ways to sharpen your focus. You need focus to put everything else aside and start working on your most important tasks. Emails may be coming in, asking you for urgent information, reminding you of promised tasks, but you put them on your to-do list and steadfastly stick to the most important task until it is complete. You need focus to concentrate hard enough and long enough on your research findings to extract insights that are actually new and useful. You need focus to be clear enough about your priorities so that you can say "no" to invitations that boost your ego but distract you from your purpose. **Having clear purpose gives you clear focus.**

If you want to be more productive, you need to become doggedly persistent in the pursuit of your goals. You need staying power to keep on working to meet your deadlines when there are more interesting things you could be doing. You may want to give up, but you keep going because of that fire in your belly that somehow gives you the energy you need to finish the job. You need staying power to pick yourself up when your paper or grant is rejected, make it better and try again. You need staying power to keep chasing your dreams when everyone around you tells you they are impossible. **Understanding your motives enables you to understand why you have to stay the course.**

If you want to increase your motivation, you need a deeper understanding of your motives. In this chapter, I will share what I've learned from the literature, and tell you how I overcame personal challenges and assumptions that were chronically disempowering, to find motives that have given me drive, focus and staying power. I want to start with a personal exploration of what I believe is at the heart of your ability to drive your career forward in the way you want, to remain clearly focused and persistently pursue your goals. I will help you better understand what fundamentally motivates you as a researcher, so that you can tap into a source of power that will enable you to achieve almost any research goal. Once you discover that power source, your next challenge is to remain connected to it. **You need to find a way to remain motivated despite the setbacks and failures that are inevitable in research.**

Smart-grid your motivation

If your motivation is what powers you, then how can you increase and maintain your motivation? The concept of the "smart grid" in energy research is a useful metaphor to explain how you can take a more purposeful and intelligent approach to create and maintain motivation in a way that flexes to the ups and downs of life. A smart-grid energy system consists of: a grid that integrates lots of different sources of local energy, usually including renewable, like wind and solar; and the smart bit. There are four things that are smart about a smart grid, and four lessons for staying motivated (Table 1). In the next four subsections, I will explain how the metaphor of the "smart grid" energy system can teach us these four lessons.

Table 1: Lessons for creating and maintaining motivation, based on the metaphor of a "smart grid" energy system

Features of a smart grid	Lesson
A smart grid flexes to the different sources available to it, storing energy when plentiful (for example on windy days) and switching to a different source when one stops producing energy (for example because there is no wind), making the supply of energy more stable and reliable.	**1.** Explore your motives to discover if you may have any hidden motives that could be demotivating or empowering you
A smart grid leaks significantly less energy than traditional systems that try and transmit the energy along long wires from distant power stations.	**2.** Reconnect with your most important motives regularly
A smart grid is more resilient to power surges and storm damage than a traditional system, as it can switch quickly to an alternative energy source to maintain an uninterrupted supply of energy.	**3.** Look for alternative motives that you can tap into when your usual sources of motivation run dry
A smart grid mainly uses	**4.** If you can't get out of a

existing energy transmission and distribution systems – you don't have to build a whole new infrastructure – you just have to think differently about what you already have.	task that is demotivating, then change the way you think about it. You don't have to find a new job if you can rediscover a new joy in your old job.

Lesson 1: Explore your motives

If you look carefully, you may discover that you have hidden motives you were previously unaware of. Some may be empowering you, while others may be demotivating you. Be aware that the things that empower and disempower you can change over time. Rather than finding a single source of motivation to rely on, try and become more aware of all the different sources of motivation you are connected to at any given time. Monitor how each given situation, relationship, goal or task makes you feel, so you can flex between different sources of motivation as some of these sources lose their power or become disempowering and demotivational. This requires a level of emotional awareness or "mindfulness" that may need practice.

For example, an invitation to contribute your expertise to a book, conference or international policy process may motivate you because it is an opportunity to make a difference or to challenge and stretch yourself, but beneath these motives may be a much more powerful motive to externally validate yourself and feel that you are somehow "good enough" as a person. When the work doesn't go according to plan, and you realise that you won't get the recognition you thought, you may suddenly find yourself wanting to give up if your ego was in fact the primary motivator. However, if you genuinely wanted to make a difference and can still do that, then you can switch to this motivation, and make a difference without getting any recognition and still motivate yourself to finish the job. If it turns out you can't even make a difference, then you may be able to switch to motivating yourself by finding the elements of the task that really stretch you, and push forward to learn the new skills you need, and enjoy finishing the task despite getting no recognition or impact.

The key to staying motivated in this example is recognising the dips in motivation that you experience as the task unfolds. By calling these dips in motivation to consciousness, it becomes possible to interrogate our motives and find new motives to continue. Alternatively, based on this analysis, we may have good reason to quit, and become empowered to provide a reasoned explanation for our discontinuation of the task. This chapter will help you become aware of the different sources of motivation available to you, so you can start switching between those different sources more intelligently, and achieve stable, high levels of motivation every day.

Lesson 2: Recharge your motivation regularly

Every now and then, something will happen that really inspires you in your work and helps you reconnect with the reasons you became a researcher. The problem is that these experiences are few and far between and the further you try to stretch that inspiration out, the more power it loses, until you find yourself running on empty most of the time. In this chapter, I will describe a number of things you can do to purposely reconnect with your most important motives and then stay connected through small actions you can take on a regular basis. Like the smart-grid energy system, you don't have to live next to a power station; you just need to find lots of smaller power sources closer to home that you can connect with on a daily basis.

For example, I started to feel really unmotivated a couple of months ago, and struggled to get myself started on any substantive work each day. I had a long list of fairly dry and unrewarding tasks that needed to be done, but I kept procrastinating, and the tasks started to pile up. I told myself that once I had done these tasks, I could reward myself with time to work on the things that I was really looking forward to. The problem was that this wasn't working, and as deadlines stacked up, my reward felt further away each day. After a couple of weeks of pushing through this fog, and getting increasingly demotivated, I switched tactic. Instead of promising myself something motivational if I could get through all the demotivating stuff, I tapped into the motivational power of the tasks I'd been reserving as a reward. Each morning, when my mind was most fresh but my motivation most weak, I focused on writing as much of this book or the next issue of my magazine as I could. By lunchtime each day, I was energised and inspired, and ready to take on that day's annoying deadline. I now only had the afternoon to nail the work for my deadline, but I powered through the work, in anticipation of the next morning's writing time. I also booked a long weekend in Shetland with my family, as I recognised that part of my problem was simply that I was tired. Our children had been ill for the majority of my last holiday and we'd spent most of our time washing clothes and sheets. I was tapping into two sources of motivation that I know are really powerful for me: writing (about things I am passionate about) and spending time with my family. By regularly recharging my motivation in these ways, I retained the focused motivation I needed to power through the other tasks on my to-do list.

Lesson 3: Find new and alternative motivations, and have a mental short cut to help you connect to them fast under pressure

A storm usually leads to a power cut because the system transmitting electricity from the power station gets disrupted, for example by the blowing down or washing away of electricity pylons, or trees pulling down wires. The power station is still producing energy, but you can't access it. You are less likely to get a power cut in a storm if you are connected to a smart grid because the grid does not depend on one single source of energy, and automatically switches to another power source. When all else fails, the "smart grid" draws on heat stored in the ground to keep you warm during the storm.

Do you have enough different motives that are sufficiently deeply held, so that you are able to automatically connect to them in the middle of the storm? In the next chapter, I will suggest some ways of finding new, values-based motives and creating powerful mental shortcuts that can enable you to access them fast when you most need them. I have found it invaluable to be able to connect instantly to my most deeply held motives at a moment's notice. It is particularly valuable when confronted with potentially career-defining decisions that have to be made quickly.

After I finished my Masters, I was offered a PhD studying tomatoes and was told that I had to decide if I would accept the offer before I had been interviewed for another PhD at the University of Leeds. The chances of being offered the Leeds PhD were much slimmer, as they were looking for a social scientist (which I wasn't) and it was a more prestigious university. The PhD in Leeds wasn't attractive on the surface of things: it included fieldwork in Africa, which I didn't see as being compatible with starting a family, and there was no funding for the fieldwork (I would have to raise this via external grants and if I failed to bring in the funds would struggle to complete my research). In this light, turning down the concrete offer seemed crazy, but when I tapped into my values-based motives (why I fundamentally wanted to do a PhD), it became clear what I needed to do. The PhD in Leeds would give me the opportunity to help communities in the Kalahari Desert, and would give me skills I could use to benefit communities elsewhere. The skills I would learn in the tomato PhD would enable me to breed tastier tomatoes[vi]. I had a choice between definite acceptance in a fully funded PhD that would generate limited impact, or possible rejection from a partially funded PhD that could generate significant impact. The decision was instantly easy, and as a result I learned how to write grants as well as a thesis during my PhD.

Lesson 4: Look at your situation differently, rather than waiting for your situation to change

Look for new ways of finding joy in old tasks and relationships; if you can't drop a role or task you no longer want, look for new reasons that will motivate you to do the things you have to do. For example, I agreed to join a research project in the first week of a new job, when I was eager to please my new colleagues. The research was outside my expertise and on a topic that doesn't interest me, and I really should have said "no". As a result, I found it increasingly hard to motivate myself to do the tasks assigned to me. However, I was committed to the project and my role wasn't going to change, so to motivate myself I had to look at the project differently. To do this, I focused on the new skills I needed to learn to make the project a success and the experience I could gain from working with colleagues from very different disciplines to generate impact with companies and publics I would never otherwise have had the opportunity to engage with. I spent time envisaging how I might be able to use these new skills and experiences in other projects, and to help others working in similar contexts. With this in mind, I found enough (just enough) motivation to complete my tasks and meet my deadlines for this project. If you can't get out of a task that is demotivating, then change the way you think about it. You don't have to find a new job if you can discover a new joy in your old job. This book is all about changing the way you think about your work.

Why are you a researcher? The power of understanding your hidden motives

I start most of my trainings with one deceptively simple question: why are you a researcher? Really, why? Stop and interrogate yourself for a moment using the questions in Box 1.

Box 1: Why are you a researcher?

Why do you do what you do? Stop for a moment and really interrogate yourself:

1. Why did you decide to do a PhD?

2. What made you apply for your first job as a researcher?

3. What did you say at your interview when they asked you why you wanted the job? What else would you have said if you were being totally honest?

4. Why do you pursue certain collaborations and not others? Do you like working with certain types of people and avoid working with others? How do these types of person make you feel and why?

5. What gets you up on a Monday morning, feeling excited about the week ahead?

6. What is most likely to give you a sense of real satisfaction and inspiration as you reflect on your day during your journey home?

People's answers often reveal more about them than they realise. Some of us are simply curious. Some of us want to achieve social standing or want our work to leave a legacy. Some of us want to make the world a better place. But when we really interrogate our motives, what lies beneath these claims?

Do you depend on the way success in your research makes you feel about yourself? Do paper and grant rejections make you doubt yourself, not only as a researcher, but also as a person? Does some inner voice tell you that you're a fake, and that you don't deserve the status of "expert"? Your latest rejection is the evidence, and surely it is only a matter of time before everyone else realises that you aren't actually that good.

Do you need recognition for your research to externally validate yourself and make you feel that you are somebody worthy of respect? Do you really seek respect from your peers or, in fact, are you using their praise to convince yourself that you can and should respect yourself? Do you want to make the world a better place so that the world can see how clever you are? Is your curiosity a way of hiding away in an enthralling world that shuts out the mundane cruelty of everyday life?

By understanding why – really why – you are researcher, you can become increasingly aware of the reasons that lie behind your motives. From a place of increasing self-acceptance and self-respect, it becomes possible to see the everyday rejections and failures of academic life as things happening around you, rather than inside you. From this perspective, you then have a choice to engage with those things deeply or let them go. Sometimes we mess up, and we need to interrogate ourselves to work out what went wrong so we can do better next time. Sometimes things are outside our control and we just need to let them pass us by.

For me, it is like seeing my life as a city full of bustling streets. I used to walk those streets blindly, with my eyes on the ground in front of me, until I would suddenly be hit by a lorry out of nowhere (my latest grant rejection or mistake). Life was unpredictable and stressful. It was impossible to escape from the background stress of life lived at street level, no matter how hard I tried to ignore the hooting horns and screaming kids. Now I live life above the city. I can see everyone else rushing around the streets, crossing roads between cars and lorries. Every now and then a lorry comes into the city for me, loaded with my latest grant rejection or error of judgement. But now rather than being knocked flat by it, I have a choice. From this height, they look more like toy cars and lorries, and I can, if I want, pick up that lorry in my hand and look at it. I am now looking at it with a sense of curiosity, wanting to understand what I need to do better next time. With a sense of calm, I then place it back on the road, and let it drive on. Sometimes, I need to really examine what went wrong, and from this perspective it is much easier to look objectively at the situation and learn useful lessons, without being blinded to what actually happened by emotional reactivity. Often it is just a reviewer with a chip on their shoulder or something that is completely outside my control. I can just put it right back on the road and let it drive off, or I can decide not to even bother picking it up in the first place. It just drives on past, packed full of all its rejection and failure, and I'm just watching, with no more than a passing curiosity.

The reality is that the reviewers and other colleagues we work with, who give us such scathing feedback, rarely intend to create emotional damage. As a handling editor for a high-ranking journal, and having served on numerous funding panels, I can tell you from experience that the reviewers aren't trying to get at you, and no one on the panel is mocking you. Every now and then, you do get reviews that are seemingly spiteful and certainly unfair, but in my experience, editors and panel members usually spot these a mile off and interpret the review accordingly. Far more frequent than the needlessly cruel review is the needlessly defensive response. The time, and more importantly, the emotional energy that has clearly been poured into that response, makes me feel deeply for the researcher every time.

The approach I have described to you is based on Relational Frame Theory, developed by Steven C. Hayes, Professor of Psychology at the University of Nevada. This theory suggests that we often take experiences out of context (such as a grant rejection), give them meaning as part of a negative story about ourselves (e.g. that we are not good enough), and then avoid thinking about these negative experiences. This "emotional avoidance" means we are unable to learn effectively from our negative experiences, and we may even find ourselves procrastinating to avoid doing things that might elicit the same negative experience again (e.g. submitting another grant proposal).

The trick, argues Hayes, is to take the bird's-eye view of the negative experience in the wider context of your professional life, recognising and letting go of the emotions associated with your latest rejection, and then refocusing on your core goals and values so you can move on, with clear focus, direction and motivation. Rather than continuing to focus on the words of the reviewers, or trying to stop feeling a particular way, you look at how those words made you feel, accept those emotions as genuine and understandable, and move on, focusing instead on your core goals and values, and what comes next. In practical terms, I have operationalised this through the ManyStory approach, described in the next chapter.

Just because you fail sometimes doesn't mean that you are a failure. Making mistakes does not mean that you are a mistake. These statements may seem both extreme and obvious, but when we examine that niggle of self-doubt, that sigh as we get back to work after a break, we may find that at some level we actually believe the reverse of these statements in our subconscious mind (that we are a failure or a mistake), despite the fact that we are so obviously incorrect. If we can become more mindful, we might be able to pick up that niggle or sigh on an emotional level, turn it over in our minds and examine it more closely. As we become more aware of our feelings, we can begin to recognise them in our conscious minds and start to separate how we feel from the experiences that life throws at us.

The next time you experience a failure or mistake in your career, if you are able to pick it up and view it like my toy lorry, rather than be flattened by your experience, you might be able to learn something important. The more fearlessly you interrogate and deal with challenging experiences and emotions linked to your work, the less afraid you will be to submit your work to the peer-review system and stop procrastinating. You will also be more likely to have learned from your previous experiences, and so you will actually get good reviews.

Over the years, I have asked many of my collaborators why they really became a researcher. Many redirected the question back to me. At first, it was easy to answer them: I was a researcher because I believed that my work could, in some small way, help make the world a better place. However, an increasing sense of self-doubt gradually crept over me, as I began to realise that my desire to make the world a better place was partly driven by a desire to somehow make up for the acts of a person who had made my world as a child so difficult. The reason it took me so long to recognise this undercurrent in my motivations was that I was afraid that my self-examination would reveal me as a fraud. At the time, I was leading a research centre, and I was terrified by the idea that I might have built this position and the years of work leading up to it on a misguided delusion of grandeur.

Two thoughts troubled me in particular. First, I wondered if I had fallen into academia because of the paint-by-numbers approach that it provides for self-esteem: work hard, get accepted in international journals, and get a pat on the back from the world. Perhaps this explained why I found it so hard when my manuscripts were rejected; if my self-esteem depended on being good enough to get published, then rejections were personal. In those days, publishing and funding success didn't just tell me I was good enough as a researcher; it told me I was good enough as a person. I took the concept of "publish or perish" to a whole new level.

The second troubling thought was that perhaps my entire career was not actually my own choice but some psychological reaction. Was I where I was because of what happened to me as a child? If so, then surely my abuser, not I, was responsible for my success. If that was the case, then I wasn't sure if I wanted to be where I was any more. The floodgates had opened.

On some subconscious level, my colleagues seemed to sense that I no longer believed in myself. One by one, they started to leave the centre. It was a cruel time. Eventually it was just me and my PA doing all the work. Then one day, I went to the printer and discovered a job application for a PA position in the local council. My PA arrived moments later to retrieve her printing, stopping short when she saw me holding her application. Rather than apologise, she told me that if I was wise, I would do the same thing. A year later, I was taking anti-depressants.

Somehow, in the midst of this darkness, I managed to find a new job. I targeted a job in a mid-ranked university that had a reputation for being friendly. My new boss allowed me to drop to a four-day week on full pay to undertake an intensive psychological recovery programme that ended up lasting almost a year.

What I realise during that year changed who I was. Rather than being ashamed of my past, I started to value many of the characteristics that had been born of it. Instead of viewing my success as evidence of dysfunction, I started to view my success as harnessing and transforming the pain I had suffered, into something good. I was retelling the story of a victim as the story of a survivor; transforming shame into victory. I was learning how to celebrate who I was in a balanced and realistic way, rather than through the temporary ego boosts of publication acceptance and funding success.

I had identified where I was leaking motivation and power: it was a story that I had told about myself. That story was consistently demotivating and disempowering me. Now, however, I was constructing a new source of motivation and power that I could tap into every day. I was rerouting my motivational smart grid, to bypass my old story that constantly leaked energy. I was retelling my story.

Key lessons

1. Motivated researchers are productive researchers

2. Motivation generates productivity for three reasons: it gives you drive, focus and staying power

3. Explore your motives to discover if you may have any hidden motives that could be demotivating or empowering you

4. Reconnect with your most important motives regularly

5. Look for alternative motives that you can tap into when your usual sources of motivation run dry

6. If you can't get out of a task that is demotivating, then change the way you think about it. You don't have to find a new job if you can discover a new joy in your old job

7. Identify behaviours that are subconsciously holding you back from submitting work for review to avoid criticism from reviewers

8. You can't learn from emotionally difficult experiences if you avoid them. Instead, recognise, process and then let go of the emotions associated with paper or funding rejections, and refocus on your core motives and values to find new direction

9. The more you do this, the less afraid you will be to submit your work to the peer-review system, and because you will have been able to learn from your previous experiences, you are more likely to get good reviews

Chapter 3
Retell your story

Even if you are broadly happy with the reasons that you are a researcher, most of us have disempowering stories we tell about ourselves from time to time. Some of us are unaware of the stories we tell about ourselves, and some of us ignore them. We do this because we are unaware of the power of these stories to demotivate us, and we do not appreciate how much motivation and energy we could gain by taking the effort to call these stories to consciousness and interrogate their veracity. Learning how to retell these stories is the most important way we can discover and embed motives based on our values, which will enrich and empower us, and so drive us, keep us focused and enable us to stay the course.

The ManyStory approach

Andrew Scott's ManyStory approach[vii] is one way of understanding the stories that hold you back and purposely retelling your story. There are three steps.

1. Loosen the grip of unhelpful stories about yourself and the people you interact with. The problem with unhelpful stories is that we have usually constructed them for a good reason, and the story will usually have been confirmed through experience. Over time, as we accept these disempowering stories, they become internalised as part of our identity. Instead of accepting that we mess up sometimes, we view our latest mistake as one in a long line of failures, both professional and personal, stretching back through the years. It feeds into a powerful meta-narrative we are telling ourselves about our lives, which disempowers us. Every now and then we succeed, or someone gives us really positive feedback, but because it does not fit into our narrative, we pay it little attention and it does not change our view of ourselves. Being aware of the stories we have constructed about ourselves is the first step to being able to consciously loosen our grip on these stories when we realise that we are feeding into them.

Phil Ward at the University of Kent created the concept of the "grant factory" as a way of helping his academics change their narrative about writing grants. Value the process of creating the grant and putting it on the conveyer belt of the peer-review process and focus on the creative process of your next grant, rather than anxiously awaiting the verdict. No matter how many times his colleagues' proposals are rejected, Phil and his team are celebrating the creative success of the grant writing process with their academics and urging them to start cooking up their next idea.

2. Discover more helpful and empowering stories linked to your values, which open up more positive possibilities for the future. If you want to believe a new story about your life, you can't just make it up. To be powerfully believable, these stories need to be based on evidence. Now you have started to loosen your grip on the unhelpful stories, it becomes possible to look across your full range of experience to find evidence that could be used to construct a more compelling and empowering narrative. The new story needs to be just as credible as the old story – if possible more credible – and it needs to be helpful. For the new story to be even more powerful than the old, unhelpful story, try and make sure that it explicitly connects with your values. This will help motivate you to push through the hard work of actually replacing the old story with the new.

A friend of mine was ready to give up research and go into university management after the latest in a long string of grant rejections. However, he decided instead to reframe his career as a thought leader, given the compelling evidence he had of his ability to write and get published in good journals. He stopped investing so much time in writing grants and started investing more time in writing and reinforcing a story he could tell himself about the unique and important contribution he was able to make to his field.

3. Enrich and embed your new story. It is hard work to replace an unhelpful story that you have told yourself again and again for years. You need to strengthen, rehearse and confirm your new story. The last step of the ManyStory approach is therefore about reinforcing the new story so that it can outcompete the old story when you are tempted to slip back into old habits. Look for as much evidence as you can find from across all parts of your life that can substantiate your new story, which you can use in future to confront your doubting self when the old story is competing for your attention. Once you have enriched the plot as much as possible, you then need to embed that plot in your consciousness, purposely telling yourself the new story, regularly, and subtly telling it to others and watching as they confirm your new narrative.

I met Ana Attlee as a PhD student and she went on to do a post-doc position with me. When I first met her, Ana was loosening her grip on a disempowering story that was being told about her by her PhD supervisor, who came from a very different scientific tradition. It turned out that she had been told a similar story again and again as she was growing up. Most PhD students would have given up under the sustained criticism she suffered, but instead, Ana was creating a new narrative, which she rehearsed again and again. It was a single sentence that was her Twitter profile text, on her website, and how she would introduce herself to people: "I'm Ana and I want to change the world." Every morning she would set her alarm for 5 a.m. and read through a number of "affirmations" she had written about herself and "visualisations" that she wanted to achieve. Then she would spend some time reading something that would help her achieve her goals, write down her thoughts, and take some exercise. She did all this before I had woken up, let alone joined her in the office. She decided that her vision was bigger than she could achieve as an academic and so set up a charity with a business to fund its work during her post-doc position with me. She now runs three highly successful businesses and through her charity is setting up a global network of urban nature reserves where poor inner-city communities can grow food. Ana enriched and embedded her new story so successfully that in a period of five years, she went from wanting to change the world to actually changing it.

How to identify unhelpful stories as they arise

The first challenge of the ManyStory approach is to identify the negative, disempowering narratives we tell about ourselves. You might be able to identify one or two of these already, as you reflect on the last section. A far greater challenge, however, is to be able to identify these narratives as they rise up out of our subconscious mind while we are going about our everyday business. If you can spot them, you can challenge them before they disempower you.

When I first started using this technique, I only tended to discover that I was lost in a train of thought long after I had been ruminating on it. I seemed incapable of spotting when my mind had wandered into a negative story, let alone being able to change the way I was thinking. I would step into my shower in the morning, deciding to meditate on a quote, and then realise as I was getting dressed that I had been thinking about the day ahead for the whole time instead. There was nothing wrong with thinking about the day ahead, but what troubled me was my inability to determine what I was thinking about, and so prepare for the day differently. Whole chunks of time were disappearing in trains of thought that I was not aware of, and sometimes these were negative, disempowering thoughts.

I am now much better at identifying these negative stories as they arise on a day-to-day basis. I have done this by becoming more aware of my body and emotions, so I can spot the first hint of negative emotion and understand where it is coming from. Despite reading numerous books and attempting various exercises, I'm still not very good at being "mindful", especially when running from deadline to deadline, as commonly happens at work. However, what I learned from the books I read left a legacy of emotional awareness that still helps me identify the first signs that I might be telling myself a negative story.

It has surprised me how frequent and insidious these stories are. To illustrate this, and show you how I spot and deal with negative stories practically, I'd like to share a mundane example of something that happened to me the other day. I went to a cash machine, on the way to the supermarket, and as I opened my wallet I noticed some receipts from a trip I'd made a month ago. I didn't look at the receipts consciously, or give them any thought, but as I put the bankcard into the machine, I noticed a slight quickening of my heart, and a kind of momentary nervousness. This passed as I took the money from the machine. A year ago, I wouldn't have even registered the change in heart rate or fleeting sense of anxiety. This time, however, as I put the money into my wallet and walked to the supermarket, I asked where that feeling had come from, and caught the beginnings of a thought process that had been triggered by seeing those receipts.

As I saw the receipts, I had been reminded of times in the past when I had sat on expenses claims for months and created huge cash-flow problems for my family. As I walked to the supermarket, I realise that I was beginning to relive the guilt and condemnation I'd felt when I had to borrow money from my parents-in-law to put food on the table, not because I was poor, but because of my incompetence at managing my expenses. That thought then led to a memory of the humiliation I had felt when I once calculated a financial figure incorrectly in a research project, and had to retract it. The bottom line, I told myself, is that I can't do simple maths – I'm stupid, irresponsible and I'm going to get me and my family into trouble someday.

These thoughts must have occurred in a flash, as I caught this story before I'd even reached the door of the shop. Previously, I wouldn't have noticed the nervousness, or the thoughts. They would have stayed buried in my subconscious mind, giving me a slight, generalised feeling of nervousness and guilt. This would have added into a background level of stress created by all the other negative stories that were swirling around, putting pressure on me.

I put the story on hold, and did my shopping. Then, as I drove home, I gave my thoughts voice, speaking aloud what I had been saying to myself to try and make the thoughts concrete enough to interrogate and challenge them. As I did this, the ridiculousness of my thought process became apparent, as well as the nuggets of truth that had given the story credibility and power in the first place.

Clearly, I am not stupid – there is ample evidence to suggest that I am highly intelligent. However, it is true that I'm not very good at maths, and I did once print and give to a number of interviewees a briefing note that contained a figure that was wrong by an order of magnitude. The negative story contained truth, but as I drove home, I reminded myself of the insights I have published, and the evidence from citations that these insights were useful to others. There were two stories; one about a Mark who is stupid and one about a Mark who is insightful. Both were based on evidence, but when I stopped to think about it, it was easy to find more evidence to support the empowering narrative.

Also, it is clear that I am not irresponsible and I am not about to put my family at risk of financial ruin. However, it is true that I have caused terrible cash flow problems for my family in the past by sitting on expenses claims. As I drove home, I imagined my wife and children playing in the garden of the house that my salary was paying for, and the holidays we've been able to enjoy together that would not have been possible without my stable income. Again, I had a choice of two alternative stories, both based on evidence, and the more I thought about the empowering narrative, the more evidence I was able to find to support a story of myself as responsible and caring.

In both cases, I didn't try and pretend that the negative story was untrue – I knew that I had messed up in the past. In both cases, I didn't try and tell an untrue story that I was in fact really good at maths or managing finances. The ManyStory approach is about recognising the fact that there are many different stories you can tell about yourself, but you have the power to choose which story you focus on. As a result, we don't ignore or deny our weaknesses, and so can take responsibility for our mistakes and deal with our weaknesses whilst telling a very different, more empowering story about ourselves.

In this case, I called to consciousness the fact that I had employed a personal assistant to deal with my expenses, and had not had a cash flow crisis since she had started working for me. Now, when my research involves numbers, I either give the job to an expert or get an expert to check my figures, and I've not made an error like that again since. I had taken responsibility for my weaknesses, and at the same time was able to tell a convincing, evidence-based story that was the opposite of the story that focused on my weaknesses. As I put the shopping away that morning, I felt inspired and empowered to get on with my day.

I have taken some time to illustrate this, because in my experience, these sorts of negative stories are incredibly common, but most people don't recognise the issue until they hear someone telling a story like this. You too may recognise that fleeting sense of nervousness or dread that you can't explain and brush under the carpet. It can be banal, and short-lived, but if you don't call what's happening to consciousness and deal with it, then you have the potential to sabotage your day without even realising it.

Finding evidence-based, empowering stories

One of the reasons that retelling your story in this way is so powerful is that you are consciously linking your narrative to your values. Your values are part of your identity, and so as we live out our new story, we reaffirm who we are, and who we want to be. In this way, we become able to connect with some of the deepest and most empowering motives that are available to us. However, it can be challenging to find a more helpful, empowering story that is based on evidence and so is believable.

To make this easier, I'd like to share a practical technique I use to help people discover more empowering stories that can motivate and inspire them. Try it out now – it is in Box 2. The result should look something like the top pie chart in Figure 1.

Based on this exercise, there are two things you can do to create an empowering story. First, turn over the piece of paper and redraw the pie chart you drew from the instructions in Box 2, this time making the size of each segment proportional to the amount of time you spend on average being that part of yourself. The result might look something like the bottom pie chart in Figure 1. Some people discover that important parts of their identity disappear from the second pie chart entirely because they never have time to spend on that part of themselves. Some people need to add new segments to their pie chart that they would rather not have to, to reflect the time spent in roles or other parts of themselves that they don't really want to be. In Figure 1, you can see how my "identity pie" differs from my time pie. The difference is much less significant now than it was the first time I did this exercise. You can see that at this point in my life, I am expressing my creative self through my research, but the time I spend working on research is squeezing out time for spiritual exploration and practice.

Box 2: Identity pie

Draw a circle on a piece of paper, and make a pie chart of all the things that make you who you are. You can try and do this in your head but it is much more effective if you actually draw it out:

- Start by simply listing (next to your circle) all the things that are part of who you are as a person. You might consider things like your gender, age, race or sexuality if these are an important part of how you see yourself. You might include roles like being a parent, a sister or a son. Perhaps part of who you are is a researcher, a mentor or a teacher. You might include characteristics such as being a perfectionist or being a caring or impatient person. You might describe part of yourself as creative or spiritual

- Now review your list and decide which are most important in defining who you are. Note that this is not who you once were or want to be, and this may have nothing to do with the amount of time you give to these parts of yourself. There may be things that are a big part of who you are, that you no longer have time to spend on, but that are still part of your identity. For example, you may still see yourself as a musician, despite the fact that you haven't picked up your instrument since you had children

- Next, put each of the most important parts of your identity into your pie chart, and make the size of each slice of the pie chart proportional to its importance as part of your identity (remember: not proportional to the amount of time you spend on it). It helps to use a pencil as you are likely to change your mind about the importance of some things as you try and fill the pie

- If you want, you can group things together to make it easier, for example, putting all your professional identities into a single slice of the pie, and your various family identities into another slice

- Consider doing this in parallel with a friend or partner, swapping your pie charts and discussing them with each other to gain further insights.

To see what this might look like, take a look at my most recent attempt at this exercise in Figure 1.

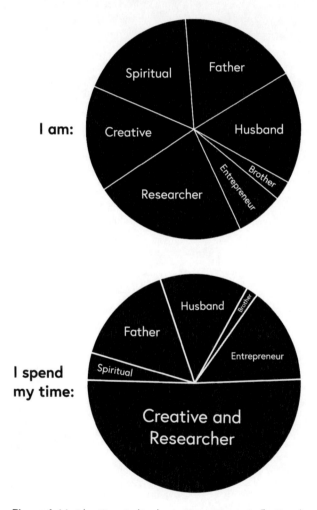

Figure 1: My identity pie (top) versus my time pie (bottom)

Second, look at both pie charts and list of all the values that underpin the different segments of your identity (where possible, write them around the outside of your pie chart, next to the segment that made you think of that value). Some of the segments may actually be values, and there may be some segments that are not underpinned by any values, but be systematic and ask yourself what values underpin each part of your identity in turn, working your way through the pie chart. If you are struggling to get to the level of values, try and think of the qualities or character traits that underpin each segment, or certain beliefs or principles. For example, when you think about your role as a researcher, you may realise how important values like honesty and integrity are to you, or as you think about your identity as a parent, how much you value patience and gentleness.

How similar or different are the first and second pie charts? If they are quite similar, you are prioritising your time in ways that are consistent with and feeding into your sense of who you are or want to be, and you probably feel fairly satisfied with your work-life balance. If the two pie charts are very different, then you probably have a sense of frustration on a fairly regular basis, and an uneasy sense of losing touch with yourself, or maybe even a fear that you may be turning into somebody you don't want to be. If the parts of your identity that are much smaller or non-existent are the parts linked to important values, then it is likely that you will feel a quite deep sense of dissonance. This dissonance is likely to actively demotivate you on a regular basis, leading to procrastination, making you question why you are doing the things you are doing, and making it harder and harder to motivate yourself.

Fortunately, this exercise provides a clear solution to this problem. You need to spend more time doing things that are aligned with your identity and values if you want to reconnect with yourself, and reaffirm (or reshape) your identity and values. If you don't, then you run the danger of becoming what you spend your time on. It won't happen overnight, but over the course of an entire career spent prioritising the wrong things, you may retire to discover you have become a different person; a person that you may or may not like.

The way you do this is by telling a new story about yourself that is based on the parts of yourself that you value most, whether or not you currently spend as much time as you would like in those parts of your identity. To embed this story in your day-to-day thinking, it needs to be an evidence-based and therefore believable story. This means that you have to actively look for evidence that you are (or at least have the potential to be) the things you value most.

The problem for many people is that they struggle to find this evidence, and so the new story is not as believable as the old, unhelpful story. For this reason, it is useful to do my pie chart exercise in parallel with someone you know well and trust, and to swap pie charts and discuss what you have done. Very often, your friend or partner is able to give you concrete examples of when you operated out of certain parts of your identity, and by discussing what they have written, you may come to realise that you share parts of your identity with them, which you had not considered explicitly before. Based on the research my colleagues and I have done, there is also another powerful reason for sharing your analysis with someone else.

I did some research recently with Dr Jasper Kenter from the Scottish Association for Marine Science and colleagues, looking at how people value nature[viii]. We wanted to understand how people value things like place identity, culture, aesthetics and spirituality as well as more practical things like places to exercise or protection from flooding. What we found went far beyond this. First, we asked people to tell us their values as individuals. Then we asked them to debate these values with others, to try and arrive at a group value. Finally, we asked them to tell us their values again as individuals, and they gave us different answers. When asked which values they trusted most, people told us they had more confidence in the values they had formed through discussion.

Our research showed that people's values are not always pre-formed – we develop and mould our values through our interactions with others. This is particularly relevant for values that we have not explored in depth before. When interrogated, we may discover that we have unconsciously adopted values on the basis of family, peer or societal norms. As a result, by explicitly discussing our values with others, we are able to better form our values, at the same time as finding evidence to support the foregrounding of these values as the basis of a more helpful story.

Rather than focusing on where you spend your time now, or what you might be becoming, you have the power to set a new course and decide who you want to be. One of the reasons that you have this power now is that you have looked and seen that these are parts of your identity, however latent, and there is evidence that you have been and can be or do all of the things you value most, even if you only ever managed to be or do something once. Once you have chosen an evidence-based new story linked to your identity and values, you can start acting out of that new identity through the smallest of first steps. Over time you can consistently show yourself that you can enact your new story, providing more evidence to support it.

We become the people we are, day by day, one decision at a time. It has taken a lifetime of decisions to become who you are today. It therefore stands to reason that retelling your story in a way that reconnects you with your most powerful, values based motives will take time. Only through sustained, consistent decisions to do the things that are most important to you, and to say "no" to the things that distract you from that ultimate purpose, can you rediscover or become the person you want to be. Your challenge, however, is to make consistent decisions in a highly inconsistent world. On a clear day, you can see the path ahead clearly, but in the midst of a storm, it is easy to become disorientated. It is often the decisions we make in the storm that we live to regret most.

Accessing empowering stories under pressure

We are often confronted with decisions under pressure. In a moment of stress, we may make a decision that further skews our time away from the things that are most important to us. Sometimes that snap decision ends up changing the course of our lives. In those few seconds, all manner of subconscious motives may rise to the surface and make us come to a decision that we end up regretting.

You need a shortcut to the lessons that you have learned about yourself; some sort of guiding principle or "motto" that you can hold in front of you at all times, ready to recall to the forefront of your consciousness as soon as you are faced with a challenging situation or decision. You are creating a direct line to your most powerful motives, which you will be able to access in the middle of the storm, no matter how disorientated and confused you might feel in the heat of the moment. Rather than powering-down at the moment you need the strongest resolve, you can connect to empowering motives that help you make decisions you feel proud of.

The final step of my exercise is therefore to look over the pieces of paper you have been working on, and sum up your identity and values in a single, memorable, empowering word, phrase, metaphor, image or motto. For this to really empower you, you need to have instant, easy access to your guiding principle. That's why it is so essential that it is short and memorable. Some people like to create some sort of visual metaphor to help them be able to instantly bring their guiding principle to mind. Some people like to commit it to memory in other ways. I have a word and a motto. The word is "empathy", which is accompanied in my mind by the image of my youngest daughter in my garden, wearing my shoes (empathy is by definition the act of putting yourself in someone else's shoes). My motto is "knowledge through love; love through knowledge". I committed it to memory during a series of walks through the forest behind my house, and I breathe in the smell of the forest and sense the winter morning sunlight through the trees as I recall it.

Finally, before you leave this chapter, reflect on the sorts of things you might want to spend your time doing, which will enable you to enact this guiding principle or motto, and affirm your identity and values. This may be about changing some of your priorities in work, but it may also be about working more efficiently so you can spend more time doing certain things outside work, which have fallen by the wayside, and which you now realise are actually really important to you.

Being a more productive researcher doesn't mean you have to produce more. Being more productive opens up the choice: to produce more; or to produce no more but get work-life balance. This leads me to what I learned from the most productive researchers in the world about how they became more productive, whilst achieving better work-life balance. In the next chapter, I will go straight to the most important lesson I learned from these researchers: prioritise.

Key lessons

1. Identify whether there are unhelpful stories you tell about yourself, either to friends and colleagues or in your head, so you can start to consciously loosen your grip on them

2. Look for evidence-based, new stories based on your strengths and achievements and linked to your values, which tell a more empowering counter-narrative

3. Work hard to replace unhelpful stories with more helpful ones. Tell your new narrative to friends and colleagues and look for new supporting evidence, so you can reinforce it and help it outcompete the old, unhelpful story

4. Reconsider how your identity as a researcher fits into your broader identity as a person, which parts of your identity link to your values and are most important to you, and how much time you spend in each part of your identity

5. Spend more time doing things that are aligned with your identity and values if you want to reconnect with yourself, and reaffirm (or reshape) your identity and values. If you don't, then you run the danger of becoming what you spend your time on

6. Make a short cut to the lessons that you have learned about yourself, summing up your identity and values in a single, memorable, empowering word, phrase, metaphor, image, motto or guiding principle, ready to call to mind when you are faced with your next big decision

7. Identify the things you want to spend your time doing that will enable you to enact this guiding principle, and affirm your identity and values

Chapter 4

Single-mindedly prioritise

By now, you should understand how your identity and values underpin your motives, and have identified new ways of thinking about your motivation that can keep you inspired and productive. You may have already summed these up in some kind of guiding principle or motto that can help inform quick-thinking, values-based decisions on a day-to-day basis. In this and the next two chapters I will draw on lessons from the literature and the researchers I interviewed and share stories that will to show you how you can turn your values into goals that inspire action.

The value-based priorities of some of the world's most productive researchers

Every one of the researchers I interviewed was a single-minded prioritiser. I say "single-minded" because they had their priorities so clearly in their minds at all times that they would not let anything else get in their way. This did not mean that they were single-minded at the expense of the people around them – quite the reverse. One of the things that surprised me most was that every researcher I interviewed talked explicitly about the values underpinning their success. They did so unprompted. I was even more surprised by the values they cited. These people were at the top of their game and revered within their disciplines, and the two most common values they cited were humility and trust.

Rather than being full of pride over their achievements, I heard stories about the importance of being approachable and open to criticism. These researchers told me how they empowered and trusted others to work effectively with them. As a result of these values, there was no heavy heart at having to break off from their work when a colleague was in crisis, because this – their team – was their work, and they did not see themselves as any more important than their most junior colleagues. They could still remember what it was like to be under the same pressures. From this place of empathy, linked to their values, helping their colleagues became a core priority.

Frede Blaabjerg, Professor in Power Electronics at Aalborg University Denmark, told me that in his mind, "there is very little difference if the person is a PhD student or a Professor. I open a conversation based on a person's research interests, not their position. People are often shy when they enter my office, but usually leave feeling that I am approachable. This is because I know that I don't have all the answers; I can admit when I don't know something". Professor Blaabjerg directs the Center of Reliable Power Electronics and is Vice President of the Danish Academy of Technical Sciences. According to Google Scholar, he has over 1000 publications, which have been cited almost 60,000 times. "Encourage and build others up", he told me. "Trust people and they rise to occasion".

Professor Gwojen Hwang has turned encouragement into a habit. "The habit of encouraging people is a key to success," he explained to me. "One needs to know that the process of publishing a paper is time-consuming and challenging. Many researchers might consider giving up a study or a paper when facing the comments from reviewers. They need encouragement as well as assistance during the research process." Professor Hwang researches e-learning at National Taiwan University of Science and Technology, and is one of three social scientists in SciVal's top 10 most prolific and cited researchers with 101 publications cited on average 20.6 times each.

It was clear that these researchers were a number of steps ahead of most of the other researchers in their disciplines, and yet they did not believe that their success made them any better than their peers. These researchers weren't undervaluing their expertise or experience, and were often called upon to provide constructive feedback and point out errors, but they did so with a spirit of humility. Cornelia van Duijn, Professor of Epidemiology at Erasmus University in the Netherlands, explained how she sometimes has to "correct other people's mistakes" but stressed, "you don't want to hurt people or imply you are superior. Humility is important; you need to tone down your superiority."

According to Elsevier's SciVal analysis, Professor van Duijn is the second most prolific and cited researcher in the world, with 195 papers cited on average 52.5 times (she has over 1000 publications if you include conference papers). She says, "I am not a person who is obsessed with power – that is not what is driving me. What I like more and more is that I see the big picture. If you don't see the big picture you can't see what the next step is for the research. It is like a jigsaw of 20,000 pieces or more, but when you are working with genes, the numbers are much greater and more complex. These are puzzles with no photograph on the box. You start with no idea how to make sense of it. We're not there but we are getting now to the point where we can start to see what is the picture. We've got 20,000 pieces coming together and we are still not quite sure what picture they are making up. That is the excitement."

Professor van Duijn spoke repeatedly about the importance of listening skills. She argued that the key to being able to listen deeply to others is humility. Without humility, our natural reaction to constructive feedback is to defend our position and so protect ourselves from the possibility that we might be wrong. Only with humility can we be fully open to the suggestions of others. By listening to advice from colleagues, she was empowered to make decisions that improved her work-life balance. Her reputation for being able to make decisions based on deep listening gave her influence as more and more people turned to her to help resolve issues: "Be humble and decisive: humility with rapid decision-making is the key to influence in a large consortium. Democratic decisions may not always be wise, but in most cases it works very well. I am often asked to be a judge in situations where people can't decide something. Maybe that's why people follow me."

One of the reasons that listening is so powerful is that it opens a channel of empathy. As Michael Nichols puts it in *The Lost Art of Listening,* "being a good listener is imagining yourself into the other person's experience." Empathetic listening doesn't require us to agree with everything the other is saying but even if we disagree, by listening with empathy the other person feels valued (their opinions are valid even if you think they may be wrong) and understood (even if you disagree with what you have understood from them). By listening, you can empower people to clarify what they think and feel, enabling them to move forward. So much of our conversation with others is in "answer machine mode", composing our thoughts while the other person speaks, just waiting for the answer machine "beep" when they finish so we can jump in with our next thought. In contrast, responsive listening, "hearing and acknowledging other people's thoughts and feelings before voicing your own", suspends your own interests for long enough to enable you to actually learn from the other person.

Carl Rogers, who worked on the "theory of the self" in the 1950s, suggested that listening can go even deeper than this. He suggested that the presence of another person who listens deeply without judgement can result in very significant transformations of the person being listened to. I learned about Rogers' work from Ioan Fazey, a Professor of Social Dimensions of Environmental Change at the University of Dundee. He wanted to develop his listening skills, so enrolled in a counselling skills course at a nearby university.

He told me, "It was kind of funny really, as I think the staff delivering the course were initially a little unsure about having me in the class – they had never had a 'professor' as a student before. But, not surprisingly, I was still a 'student' – and my expertise was not as well developed as theirs in the skill of listening. I was truly learning from them about the skill of listening and how this can result in the transformation of others. This experience highlighted two things for me. First, I realise that I needed to learn to develop my skills as a listener, and the fact that I was an expert in my academic world had no bearing on my skills as a listener/counsellor. Second, it surprised me how transformative listening can be. I hadn't anticipated this."

Rogers' work led to the development of "person-centred therapy" and "learner-centred teaching", focusing on the role of listening to facilitate personal growth and learning, rather than directly telling a person how to grow or learn. By suspending your own judgment and assumptions as you listen, you enable the person speaking to express and become all that they have the potential to become.

Finally, the researchers I interviewed appeared to have a presence of mind that enabled them to resist the mental urge to correct embarrassing but inconsequential mistakes, have the last word or be seen to be right if it meant humiliating their colleague. Instead, these researchers are travelling an alternative path that rises above the petty point-scoring of much academic debate, to see the bigger picture. Despite spending years painstakingly piecing together their particular puzzle, these researchers are prepared to start again if it becomes clear that they are wrong. "You need to hold lightly to your own views, and trust your team," explained Kee Hung (Mike) Lai, Associate Professor in the Department of Logistics and Maritime Studies at Hong Kong Polytechnic University. Professor Lai is an editor of three international journals and on the editorial board of four others. According to Google Scholar, he has >200 publications since 2001 (including seven books), which have been cited >11,000 times. He told me: "The one most important thing you can do if you want to be productive as a researcher is trust in your team members. If you trust the other person's judgment you can save yourself a lot of time by acting on their advice. As a researcher, I know how much I don't know, which makes it easy to trust and act on the knowledge of my team. Have an attitude of gratitude and think positive, even if you are being criticised; try and address their comments rather than fighting them. In Chinese, we say *guan xi* or 'harmony'. We can be productive because we don't argue; we are using the time others spend arguing being productive."

One of the reasons these researchers were able to hold their priorities so clearly in front of them at all times may be because they came from the heart, not the head. If I were to ask you to write a list of work priorities right now, there is a good chance that you might struggle to recall them all if I asked you to do the same thing a month or two from now. If instead, you look to see what priorities are already in your heart, linked to your most important values, you will be able to look again in a couple of months' time and see exactly the same priorities. In the same way, the researchers I interviewed were able to tell me their priorities instantly, without hesitation, and had been pursuing them consistently for years.

The methods that these researchers were using to prioritise their work were not particularly novel or radical. What was both new and challenging for me was the way these researchers thought about their priorities, in particular how strongly they were connected to their values. In the midst of these profound insights, my interviews identified a number of interesting methods and pieces of advice that are also worth sharing, for example:
- Make every two hours count, whether for work or play: "I manage my time by dividing it into two-hour blocks, including holding group meetings, reviewing papers, discussing with students, listening to music and watching TV" (Gwojen Hwang)
- Make every second of work time count when you are in the office if you don't want to be working when you get home (Kee Hung (Mike) Lai)

- Have a small number of high priorities that you prioritise every day: "PhD students have to come first – teaching is my major priority. Number two is publishing in top journals. I have a small number of high priorities that I make sure I prioritise every day" (Kee Hung (Mike) Lai)
- Make a strategic plan for your day, and don't do a task you "should" do (like email) as long as there is a more important unfinished task linked to your core goals: "I start before 07.00 and work without emails or distraction, making strategic decisions about goals for my day and getting any urgent and important things done efficiently." (Frede Blaabjerg)
- Prioritise being a good collaborator so opportunities continue coming your way: "my top priority is giving feedback to colleagues as a co-worker quickly and not delaying my part in the work, and then people want to continue working with me." (Frede Blaabjerg)

Humility is rare in academia, but when you combine humility with exceptional talent and expertise, you get a research leader. These are not the traditional leaders who lead from the front, name-dropping and subtly boasting their credentials at any opportunity, pushing their teams to the limit and defending themselves against criticism as though their lives depended on it. These are quiet leaders. They lead from behind, sharing credit for success with their colleagues, trusting and empowering their teams and learning from criticism. These are people whose teams others want to join, and whose collaborators keep returning with new opportunities. Success is more rather than less satisfying when it is shared, and when it is not achieved at the personal expense of others. If you seek values-based goals rather than seeking to be productive, productivity becomes a by-product of seeking your goals.

Setting values based goals

The researchers I interviewed were able to single-mindedly prioritise their goals because they were clearly linked to their values. If you want to set goals that stick with you for years and motivate sustained action, you need to start with your values. To do this, try the exercise in Box 3.

Your answers to the three questions in bold at the end of Box 3 will provide you with prototype goals that are explicitly linked to your values. At this stage, they might be quite conceptual, and it may difficult to see how you would actually realise them. Therefore, the next step is to turn these into SMART goals that you can actively pursue on a day-to-day basis.

Box 3: How to set values-based goals

To identify prototype goals that link to your values, try the following steps:

1. Revisit your identity pie chart and shortcut to your core values from the previous chapter

2. Look at the words and phrases you wrote during that exercise, and rearrange them in your mind or on the page to form an overarching goal that connects some of the most important parts of your identity and values to a desired future state. For example, this could be a dream job, a place you now live in, who you are with, who you have become or some other future state of being

3. Visualise yourself in this future state, in as much detail as possible. Imagine a day in the life of your future self. Where are you eating breakfast? What does it taste like? What are you thinking as you go to work? What is your office like? Who are you working with? What emotions do you feel? How do the people around you feel? Try and use as many of your senses as possible to imagine your future state

4. Finally, compare this to a couple of representative days in your current life and ask which aspects are most similar and which are dissimilar to the future you have imagined:

o   Do you ever get glimpses of that ideal future? What are you doing when this happens? **How could you do more of this?**

o   Are there things in your current reality that are already taking you to that future? Personality traits, processes or actions? **How could you build on these?**

o   What aspects of your current reality are furthest (or taking you) away from your ideal future? **Which of these can you do something about?**

Key lessons

1. Become a single-minded prioritiser who practices humility, empathy and trust

2. Empower, encourage and trust others to work effectively with you and they will rise to the challenge and create shared success

3. Practise empathy with your colleagues, making the effort to imagine yourself in their shoes, no matter how different they or their situation might appear

4. Practise humility by listening deeply to your colleagues, suspending your own interests for long enough to actually learn from them

5. Don't do a task you "should" do (like email) as long as there is a more important unfinished task linked to your core goals

6. Identify priorities linked to your values that you can turn into more concrete goals

7. If you seek values-based goals rather than seeking to be productive, productivity becomes a by-product of seeking your goals

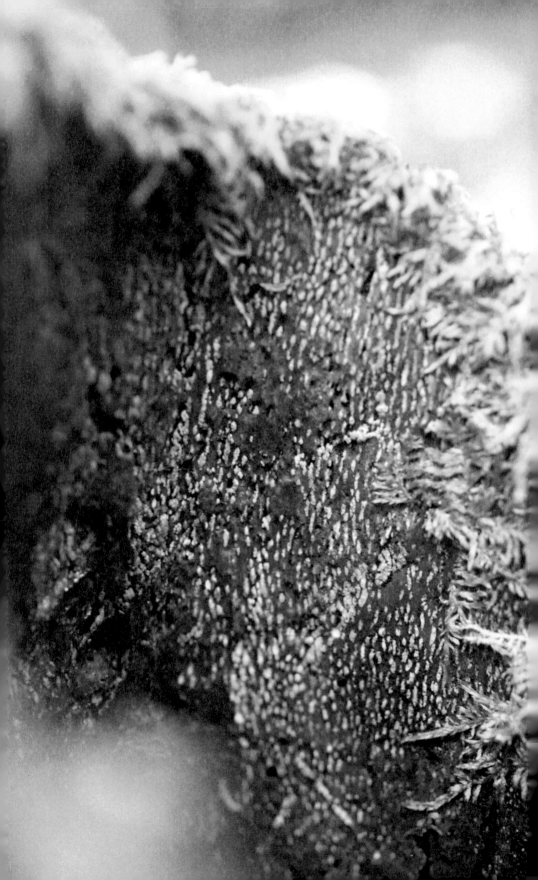

Chapter 5
Find goals that inspire you: the new SMART

Many of us have been told at some point in our career that goals should be Specific, Measurable, Achievable, Realistic and Timely (SMART). This is a good start, but from listening to the researchers I interviewed and reading the research literature, I have discovered a more empowering and evidence-based approach. I now create goals that are Stretching, Motivational, Authentic, Relational and Tailored: the new SMART. In this chapter, I will explain the theory behind this new type of goal, and ask questions that will help you identify your own goals more powerfully than you have conceived of them previously.

You can create SMART goals for your work and personal life. For example, I have two linked work and personal goals that I have developed to be SMART. My first goal is to lead a grassroots revolution that changes the way researchers generate and share knowledge, so that their ideas can change the world. The linked personal goal is to achieve this without being away from home more than two nights a week, and never working evenings or weekends when I am at home. In the next chapter, I explain how I developed this goal, and how you can put your own SMART goals to work for you in practice.

1. Stretching goals

Edwin Locke and Gary Latham summarised 35 years of empirical research on goal-setting theory in their 2002 article in *American Psychologist*, "Building a Practically Useful Theory of Goal Setting and Task Motivation". They found that the most difficult goals led people to produce the highest levels of effort and performance. Their meta-analysis showed a direct, linear correlation: the more difficult the goal, the more effort and performance they measured, until they reached the natural limit of human ability for the given task. People who set stretching goals were between 60 and 70 per cent more likely to achieve higher levels of effort and performance than those who just tried to "do their best".

The reason for this, they argued, was that there is no concrete reference point for a person's "best". Therefore, a range of levels of effort and performance could be considered to be acceptable as a person's "best" under the circumstances. At first, they wondered if it was the lack of specificity that prevented these people from reaching their potential, but when these people were asked to set specific goals, there was no discernible difference. The reason for this was that people set a wide range of specific goals, from realistic to stretching. It was the people who set stretching goals that showed the greatest "effect size" in their analysis.

Questions:

- How much do your current goals stretch you?

- What if you multiplied them by four or asked yourself if you could achieve them in a quarter of the time, and really turned your mind to how you might achieve it?

- Might you come up with a whole new approach, and might you actually get there?

Even if you only get part of the way there, Locke and Latham's research suggests that your progress will bring you rewards (such as external recognition or an internal sense of satisfaction), which will increase your confidence and sense of self-efficacy, which will in turn increase the likelihood that you build on your progress to get even closer to your goal. **So, the first step to develop a new SMART goal is to stretch yourself.**

2. Motivational goals

Some people are motivated by the very fact that their goals stretch them. Stretching goals can, however, be demotivational if they are unrealistic. For example, if you set yourself the stretching goal of learning to fly unaided, you would realise before you hit the ground that you had reached and surpassed what is humanly possible. Even if you set yourself a goal that is theoretically possible but extremely stretching, such as travelling to outer space, then you might become so intimidated by the goal that you never take the first step towards achieving it. Rather than being inspired to action, you might be debilitated by the fear of failure, judging your current position and performance in terms of how far you are falling short of your goal.

The solution, argue Locke and Latham, is to focus on what you need to learn to be able to reach your goal, and to turn these learning goals into milestones that progressively take you closer to your stretching goal. They review research showing how people who focus on learning goals tend to perform better than those who focus on performance goals. As a result of this learning, new ways of reaching your goals may become clear, and you may gain new competencies and awareness that enable you to exploit opportunities to reach your goals in creative new ways, which you might otherwise have missed. Now, instead of focusing on whether you are any closer to space travel and being disappointed that your dream is still far beyond your reach, you focus on whether you gained one of the skills you know you will need if you want to be able to travel into outer space.

By using this example, I am alluding to the story of Peter Diamandis, who founded the X Prize for private space travel. He was passionate about space and wanted to become an astronaut when he grew up. By the age of 12, he had won a rocket design competition at school, and at university he made friends with people who worked for NASA. He was doing research in the lab one day when some of his NASA friends visited him with an application form for getting into NASA to train as an astronaut. They told him that his chances of getting selected were 1 in 1000, and if he got selected, then "maybe" he would fly, and if he flew, he might fly once or twice in his entire career. He decided that day that he would get into space without NASA.

He had read a book about the plane called the *Spirit of St. Louis* which made the first solo non-stop transatlantic flight, piloted by Charles Lindbergh in 1927, for which he won the $25,000 Orteig Prize. Diamandis figured that a prize of $10M might be enough to incentivise someone to realise his dream to travel to space. So, he established the X Prize for the first private company who could put a person into space and return them safely to earth again – twice. The only problem was that he didn't have any money.

After a year of fundraising, he had only managed to raise half a million, but instead of giving up, he decided to launch his $10M prize anyway, convinced that it was just a matter of time before someone caught his vision and fully funded the prize. The launch took place at the site where the *Spirit of St. Louis* took off in 1927, and he shared the platform with his astronaut friends from NASA. The story made the front page of newspapers around the world. It took him five years, after speaking to over 150 CEOs, before the Ansari Family rose to his challenge, and he renamed it the Ansari X Prize in their honour. In the meantime, the competition had inspired 26 teams from seven different countries to enter, and the competition was won in 2004 by Mojave Aerospace

Ventures. The winning vehicle, SpaceShipOne, was piloted to space twice within two weeks to win the competition, and now hangs in the National Air and Space Museum next to the *Spirit of St. Louis*.

Rather than being demotivated by the odds that his NASA friends spoke of in the lab that day, Peter Diamandis focused on what he needed to learn in order to realise his dream a different way. He spent the first few years of his new journey learning how to fundraise and create publicity on a global scale, eventually coming up with a solution to his $10M problem based on an insurance policy that was underwritten by the Ansari Family. He has since applied what he learned to fund prizes to incentivise step changes in health and education, among other goals.

Often the thing that holds us back is not a lack of resources or ability, but a lack of ambition. We need aspirations that are inspirational enough to push us to the next level of thinking and action. **The second step to developing a new SMART goal is to find highly motivational goals.**

Questions:

- Do your goals inspire and motivate you?
- If not, can you link your goals more effectively to your values (see the previous section on values-based goal-setting) or stretch your goals in other ways that will make them more motivational?
- Can you make your most stretching goals more motivational by breaking them up into a series of learning goals?
- What new knowledge, skills, networks or capabilities do you need to achieve your most stretching goals?
- What do you need to learn before you will be able to achieve them?
- What is the first thing you need to know and how can you learn about it?

3. Authentic goals

For your goals to be authentic, you need to set them yourself so they genuinely represent your aspirations, and you believe in your ability reach them (the concept of "self-efficacy"). Locke and Latham showed that those with higher self-efficacy set higher goals than people with lower self-efficacy, were more committed to their goals (whether they set them themselves or were assigned goals by a manager), found more effective strategies for reaching their goals, and were more likely to respond well to negative feedback.

Most researchers have the luxury of being able to set their own goals (most of the time). Increasingly, however, I hear researchers complaining about various targets and goals being imposed externally on them by managers. In response, I hear two common strategies: burying your head in the sand and ignoring your managers (which works surprisingly well in academia) or translating externally imposed goals into more authentic, self-set goals that you actually want to achieve. For example, getting published in a top journal and becoming highly cited is a common self-set goal among more competitive researchers, which typically corresponds well to goals set by managers in relation to assessments of research quality or global rankings.

Professor Lai told me, "In Hong Kong, academia is becoming more competitive, with annual appraisals and peer pressure increasingly driving people. I work with high-performing researchers in a high-performing institution. When everyone is working at such a high level, it pushes you forward."

Being authentic doesn't mean I have to rebel against the norms of my peers or the expectations of my managers (although that is, of course, the academic prerogative). Instead, I look for win-wins where I can pursue authentic goals that also meet some of the key needs of the colleagues I work with. For example, in my own institution, I am expected to bring in research money, yet I could do much of my research without significant funding. More authentic for me than pursuing funding is the pursuit of benefits for society. However, by trying to achieve these goals primarily in the context of funded research projects, I have discovered that I have the resources I need to generate higher quality evidence and more significant and far-reaching impacts than I could have otherwise achieved, whilst meeting the aspirations of my department.

Self-efficacy can be a real challenge for many researchers. Researchers are already among the most educated people in the world. Yet, many find it hard to believe that they deserve the "expert" label that is put on them by the media, their students and peers. High-achieving individuals who are unable to accept or internalise their accomplishments are often said to experience the "imposter phenomenon". Sufferers have a tendency to dismiss evidence of competence as luck or the result of having deceived others into thinking that they are more competent than they really are. Accordingly, they live in constant fear of being exposed as a "fake". While some researchers live in this reality for much of their working life, it is more common for researchers to doubt their self-efficacy on a more reactive basis, for example, after negative feedback or failure.

Kumar and Jagacinski, writing in the journal *Personality and Individual Differences* in 2006, reviewed literature showing that people who worry about being an imposter tend to report higher levels of anxiety, perceive they are less competent than their peers, do not expect to perform well and have more negative reactions to failure than people who do not experience the phenomenon. These fears prevent them from aiming as high as their potential. In some cases, the imposter phenomenon results in self-sabotage, for example, procrastinating over the submission of an article that is never perfect and so never gets submitted and avoids attracting any negative feedback. If you recognise these thoughts and feelings, take a look again at Relational Frame Theory and the ManyStory approach in Chapters 2 and 3.

Whether or not you would describe yourself as an impostor, self-doubt may still be preventing you from setting authentic goals that represent your true aspirations. You need to believe in yourself before you can allow yourself to dream of the positive things you might do. Only then can you articulate these positive things as goals (as opposed to the negative things you might do, which you may articulate as worries). **The third step is to avoid adopting someone else's goals, and instead develop your own goals which are authentic to your dreams and abilities. Find personal strengths you can believe in, and build your goals on this concept of self-efficacy.**

Questions:

- Did you set the goals you are currently pursuing yourself, or were they given to (or imposed on) you?

- If you have to chase goals for your institution or manager, are there goals that you can set for yourself that you can believe in, which may also enable you to get closer to your institution's goals?

- Do you sometimes feel like a fake, and does this stop you from dreaming big?

- Can you find an alternative, evidence-based and more empowering narrative that empowers you to set authentic goals that genuinely represent your aspirations and which you believe you can achieve?

4. Relational goals

The researchers I interviewed for this book all had goals that were based on their values. The values that their goals were based upon all shared one common characteristic: they were other-regarding, rather than self-regarding. If you want to set relational goals, consider how your goals interact with the goals of others around you and affect them, and how achieving your goals might provide win-wins for people who are important to you.

For example, you may need to achieve your goals as part of a team. The first element of a relational goal in this context would be understanding the strengths and motives of your team members in order to delegate to, or request help from, those who are likely to gain most themselves from helping you achieve your goals. The second element of a relational goal in this context would be articulating and agreeing your goal with the team, and then being accountable to the group for your progress towards each of the learning (rather than performance – see "stretching goals" above) milestones you set for yourself on your journey towards your ultimate goal. If you are working alone towards your goals, you might want to think about the knock-on benefits for your immediate colleagues or your family if you were to reach your goal, so you are working towards something that is other-regarding, rather than just self-regarding, and so more likely to stand the test of time, through those wobbly moments when you don't regard yourself as highly as you ought to.

The most powerful goals are often intrinsically other-regarding. Living life in service to goals that are purely self-seeking can become one-dimensional and emotionally draining over time, compared to goals that seek to benefit others, which emotionally energise and inspire. One researcher described the need to turn encouragement into a "habit", while another told me how he empowered colleagues by simply putting his trust in them to do important tasks in his team. Professor Gwojen told me about the need to adopt "a selfless attitude, sharing ideas with others, building trust, and most importantly learning from them". He was warned that his open, sharing attitude could get him into trouble: "A colleague once asked me, 'Aren't you afraid that someone might copy your ideas and do the same research as yours?', but I answered, 'that will encourage me to find more and better research topics'".

Goal-setting is usually an exclusively self-centred exercise. However, the researchers I interviewed turned traditional logic on its head and set goals that deliberately built up others in their teams, rather than themselves. They did this because of their regard for the others in their team, rather than doing it out of regard for themselves. Yet, as a result of the other-regarding nature of their goals, their teams respected and gave back to them, powering them to success.

It could be argued that the limited "social distance" between these researchers and their teams made it easier for them to pursue goals that regarded the needs of their team members, compared to people outside their institution or discipline. We know that people tend to find it easier to behave altruistically towards others with whom they empathise, interact with regularly, or who they perceive are socially similar to them, for example in gender, class or ethnicity. Having said this, no matter how easy it might be to set relational goals in theory, it is difficult in practice to remember the needs and aspirations of those around us when we think about our future. **The fourth step is to develop relational goals that are other-regarding rather than self-regarding. Consider how achieving your goals could create win-wins for others around you.**

Questions:

- How self- or other-regarding are your goals?

- Might the achievement of any of your more self-regarding goals have a negative impact on others?

- How might others benefit when you achieve your goals?

- What single thing could you do that would have the greatest positive impact on the people you work closely with?

5. Tailored goals

Finally, SMART goals need to be tailored to your unique identity and strengths. The more effectively you tailor your goals to your values and abilities, the more likely you are to set authentic goals that are stretching enough, motivating and genuinely relational.

There are two parts to this. The first part is to make sure your goals build on, consolidate or enact your values and identity, rather than taking you further away from them. If you completed the pie chart exercise in Chapter 3, you should have a detailed picture of your values and identity that you can build on.

The second part is to tailor your goals to your unique strengths and capabilities. Goals are often designed to solve problems or address weaknesses. However, focusing on problems and weaknesses can be disempowering, feeding into the negative stories that we (and others) construct about us. I am not encouraging you to disregard, disown or hide from your weaknesses and failings. To do so would clearly be unbalanced and unhealthy. However, it is possible to accept and be aware of our weaknesses, while choosing to focus on our strengths (I'll discuss this in greater detail in Chapter 6). Reviewers and colleagues will remind us of our failings on a regular basis anyway. For

67

most researchers, the greater challenge is to construct, evidence and embed positive stories about ourselves that can empower and motivate us (see the ManyStory approach in Chapter 3). **The final step, therefore, is to tailor your goals to your unique values and abilities. Make sure your goals build on, consolidate or enact your values and identity, rather than taking you further away from who you are or want to be. Make sure your goals build on your strengths, seeking these out and reminding yourself of your capabilities as you seek your goals.**

Questions:

- To what extent do your goals take you away from, build on, consolidate or enact your values and identity?

- What is important to you about your current situation that you want your goals to protect and build on?

- What is the next level of thinking you need to reach for you to be able to look differently at your options?

- What question, if answered, could make the most difference to your future situation?

- What would it take to catalyse change at an unprecedented pace or scale?

- Who can you reach out to who could enable you to make a step change in your progress?

- If success was guaranteed and you had no limitations, what would you try doing?

Not all goals are created equal

The research evidence clearly suggests that goals with certain characteristics are more likely to be achieved and drive high performance. Although not a scientific validation of these findings, the experiences of the researchers I interviewed illustrate the power of single-mindedly prioritising goals that explicitly link to your values. Values-based goals that are Stretching, Motivational, Authentic, Relational and Tailored can drive sustained action. These are not like other goals you might have set yourself in the past. You have imbued them with the unique power of your most important values. These are therefore goals that you care deeply about. They are the sorts of goals for which people will make deep personal sacrifices. They are the sorts of goals that can mobilise teams and continue motivating you when all else seems lost. Ultimately, they are goals that happen.

Key lessons

1. Develop goals that stretch you. Even if you only get part way there, your progress will bring you rewards that will increase your confidence and sense of self-efficacy, which in turn will increase the likelihood that you build on your progress and get even closer to your goal

2. Make goals that motivate you. Often the thing that holds us back is not a lack of resources or ability, but a lack of ambition. We need aspirations that are inspirational enough to push us to the next level of thinking and action

3. Don't adopt someone else's goals; instead, develop your own goals which are authentic to your dreams and abilities. Find personal strengths you can believe in, and build your goals on this concept of self-efficacy. People who believe in themselves set higher goals that they are more committed to, find more effective strategies for reaching their goals, and are more likely to respond well to negative feedback when things don't go according to plan

4. Develop goals that are other-regarding rather than self-regarding. Consider how achieving your goals could create win-wins for others around you. Living life in service to goals that are purely self-seeking can become one-dimensional and emotionally draining over time, compared to relational goals that seek to benefit others, which emotionally energise and inspire

5. Tailor your goals to your unique values and abilities. Make sure your goals build on, consolidate or enact your values and identity, rather than taking you further away from who you are or want to be. Make sure your goals build on your strengths, seeking these out and reminding yourself of your capabilities as you seek your goals

6. Values-based goals that are Stretching, Motivational, Authentic, Relational and Tailored can drive sustained action. You care deeply about them and so they happen

Part 2: **Making it happen**

Chapter 6
Plans that work

In this second part of the book, I want to take the principles from the first part and show how you can apply them practically to turn your new-found motivation and goals into powerful values-based actions. As with the first part of the book, I will do this through a mix of lessons from the literature (drawing from a broader range of disciplines than is normally brought to bear on these issues), my own experience and the experiences of those I interviewed for the book.

Mind the value-action gap

Values-based goals that meet my new SMART criteria can be inspirational, but they may not automatically inspire action. There is a well-known gap between people's stated goals and values, and the actions they actually take. We don't like to admit it, but most of us are hypocrites to some extent. For example, I do research on environmental issues and have a set of values and aspirations based around protecting the environment, and yet I fly on average once a week, and so have a larger carbon footprint than almost anyone I know.

A number of causes and solutions have been proposed to bridge the value-action gap[ix]. Some say that if I could just be made more aware of the consequences of my actions, I would start to align my actions better with my values and fly less. Others would suggest that my actions are more influenced by peer pressure and a desire to conform to social norms than they are by my values (I can argue that all researchers travel the world to collect data and present at conferences, including those who study climate change). Others would focus their attention on helping me to find practical strategies and opportunities to take action. They would look for incentives and resources that would make action more likely. They might persuade me to make a public commitment to action or encourage me to seek positive feedback from peers to reinforce and sustain positive actions to reduce the number of flights I take.

I have tried many of these approaches, without success. This is because there is one simple reason for my flight-taking environmental hypocrisy. My travel choices force me to make a trade-off between an extra day or night away from my wife and young children or taking a flight, and the values that underpin my love for my family motivate me more than the values that underpin my love for the environment. I have stopped feeling guilty and berating myself for not having values that align with those of my environmentalist colleagues (who are often single, have grown-up children or just have different priorities). Instead, I have learned to accept that these are my priorities at this point in my life, and I am focusing on reducing my carbon footprint in other ways.

The point I am trying to make is that you achieve the goals you value most. Rather than trying to change your values, understand the values that are most important to you, and find goals that arise from these values. Having said this, although it is easier to achieve goals linked to your most important values, you may still disappoint and frustrate yourself by not taking the time or the steps you know you need to take. The value-action gap is real, and I do not know anyone who consistently acts in line with their values. So don't be too hard on yourself, and don't give up. The next section will show you how you can start to make systematic, steady progress towards your goals using what I have learned from the study of behaviour, organisational and systems change, international development and ecology.

Three questions to turn intention into action

If you have SMART, values-based goals, then the behaviour change research I summarised at the start of the previous section offers a number of ways to bridge the value-action gap. Based on this body of work and broader research on achieving change in organisations, socio-technical systems, ecosystems and international development, a number of practical strategies and approaches have been devised. Each has its own jargon and internal logic, which can get confusing. Therefore, instead of reviewing the strengths and weaknesses of each approach, this section synthesises the best bits of them all into three simple questions you can use to turn your goals into action.

The methods I have drawn upon are not exhaustive, but represent some of the most widely used and highly cited approaches, including: logic models like Theory of Change and Logical Framework Analysis, which are typically used in international development; the Goals, Reality, Options, Will (GROW) model from the coaching literature; and strength-based methods from the organisational change literature, like Appreciative Inquiry and the strengths, opportunities, aspirations and results (SOAR) framework.

To turn your goals into action, answer these three questions:

- What works?
- What will you do?
- How will you know it worked?

1. What works?

Start by compiling an evidence-base comprising: i) your own strengths, capabilities and successes; and ii) evidence of what has enabled others like you to achieve similar goals.

Most people start by identifying the problems they need to overcome in order to reach their goals, but this can be a profoundly discouraging experience, depending on the number of barriers you identify. You may discover that there are many more barriers than you anticipated, both external and internal. If you asked highly successful individuals whether they would have started on the journey that took them to success, had they known the magnitude of the challenges they would face, many would tell you that they would never have started. Focusing on the external barriers may make you give up entirely on your goals. Focusing on the internal barriers can be equally disempowering for other reasons. As you focus on your limitations and weaknesses, your confidence is weakened, and you are likely to perceive the external barriers as being greater and more insurmountable than you previously thought.

In contrast, asking "what works" turns problem-solving on its head. By asking this question, you are shifting your focus from the barriers between you and your goals to the unique strengths and capabilities you can use to achieve your goals. By doing this, you turn barriers (e.g. I don't have the right skills) into opportunities (e.g. I know someone who has the right skills or I would like to learn how to do this myself), and transform the disempowerment of problem-solving into an empowering exploration of what works and might be possible. For many people, this exploration can be uncomfortable. With the exception of applying for a job, few people are accustomed to assessing their strengths and capabilities, and find it difficult to be objective.

To make this easier, consider your strengths and capabilities in different domains. Most people start with knowledge and skills. However, you can also consider experiences of success in the past, analysing what worked and why. More challenging, and more likely to be overlooked, is the domain of power. In addition to the knowledge, skills and experience that you can draw upon to achieve your goals, you will have certain levels of hierarchical, social, personal and transpersonal power that you can use.

Find someone who knows you well and respects you (e.g. a close friend or partner) and complete the power questionnaire in the Appendix for yourselves, and then for each other, and compare your scores. Grade your power specifically in relation to your ability to achieve your goals, bearing in mind that if you have very different goals, you may have to repeat this for each goal. For example, as a professor I may have a lot of hierarchical power to achieve a career-based goal within my own institution, but this position may significantly limit my power within a group of stakeholders I want to influence who are deeply sceptical of academic experts.

Critics of the "what works" approach argue that it encourages people to avoid looking at what doesn't work or the barriers, leading to inflated egos, simplistic solutions and unintended consequences. These are valid points if the approach is taken to an extreme, and some people do take it too far. We have all seen people with inflated egos who are blind to the carnage they create in relationships all around them as they focus on their success to the exclusion of any admission of failure or weakness. This narcissistic behaviour is typically a mechanism to cope with unbearable feelings of weakness or shame, projecting these characteristics onto others in order to focus on the parts of themselves they are able to love. Narcissists don't need to learn how to focus on their successes, but most normal people find it useful to be reminded of what has worked for them in the past. Colleagues and reviewers will constantly remind us of the weaknesses in our work, and failure (e.g. to publish or win funding) is a hallmark of academic life. If you find it easier to focus on the negatives than you do to focus on your successes, then asking yourself "what works" can be a useful counter-balance to your dominant narrative. Your failures and weaknesses will remain in view, but they will now be framed in the context of a much more empowering narrative.

2. What will you do?

You know what has worked in the past and the successes and strengths you will build on, but this empowering narrative now needs clear direction. You need to start on a path that will take you to your goals. I have developed an approach to embark on systematic action to reach my goals, based on theories and methods from a range of disciplines. Figure 2 breaks this down into a number of achievable steps, and the text that follows will illustrate each step with an example of how I have used it to help me realise my own professional goals.

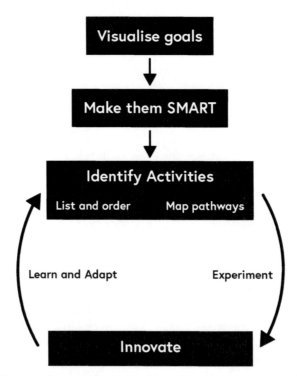

Figure 2: Four steps to take achievable action towards goals

I will allude to the disciplinary roots of each step where possible but will not go into great depth, as I have heavily adapted and integrated these theories and methods over the years, and I want to make the steps as easy-to-follow as possible.

2.1 Visualise your goal(s) in as precise detail as possible: see Chapter 4 for visualising values-based goals. For example, visualising my goal of training researchers around the world, I might imagine myself waking up in Australia, eating breakfast with my family on a hotel terrace and thinking of all the researchers between the UK and Australia that I have trained and who are now achieving impacts from their research. I can smell the sea and I have an overwhelming sense of gratitude.

2.2 Make them SMART: work though Chapter 5 to make your goals as Stretching, Motivational, Authentic, Relational and Tailored as possible. For example, my SMART goal is "to lead a grassroots revolution that changes the way researchers generate and share knowledge, so that their ideas can change the world". Don't worry if your goal grows arms and legs in this process. You can list additional goals as they arise, or break your goal up into a series of smaller goals. For me, the travel required to achieve this goal is not consistent with my family-centred values, so I set myself an additional personal goal of achieving my goal of training researchers (above) without ever having to be away from home more than two nights a week, and never working evenings or weekends when I am at home.

2.3 Identify activities that will enable you to reach your goal. There are two ways you can do this:

i) List and order: I usually take the simpler of the two approaches, and just list activities I will do, trying to be as comprehensive as possible, and sorting them into a vague order. This drastically simplifies the "logic model" approach. It is probably not as powerful as the full approach where I would identify "inputs" to my activities (e.g. staff or money), and outputs (e.g. people trained) and outcomes (e.g. impacts achieved by those I train) from my activities, which are staging posts on the pathway to my eventual goal. However, from my experience of training in this approach, I know that people get tied up in knots trying to work out the difference between inputs, activities, outputs and outcomes, rather than just focusing on what they need to do to achieve their goals. My approach may be a little more haphazard, but it keeps things simple and quick, which is why I use this technique. In my example, the main activity is training as many researchers as I can around the world in my empathic, relational approach to research impact. To do this without spending my life travelling, I know that I have to franchise the company at some point in the future, and to promote my approach and generate demand for training I am creating a free product ecosystem, including my podcast, magazine, blog and free online impact training for researchers.

ii) Map pathways: If you want to take things further, I would recommend the "theory of change" approach, in which you map the different pathways you could take to get you from where you are now to your goals (Figure 3). Starting with your goal, backtrack systematically to identify the activity or achievement that is most likely to immediately precede your goal, and then work out what would precede that. Like a map, there are always multiple routes you can take to get to any destination. Rather than trying to find the fastest or most scenic route, you map out a few different routes to start with, so you can evaluate which ones are most likely to get you to your destination.

Do this one step at a time, working backwards from your goal. What are the things that would have to happen immediately preceding reaching your goal, and what step would precede this? If your goal is to solve a problem, you may need to follow this process right back to the root cause of the problem over many steps.

Figure 3 shows a Theory of Change developed by the Fiver Children's Foundation to reach the goal of children in their care growing up to be "happy and fulfilled in work, family and life and make positive contributions to society". When I created my first personal Theory of Change, I identified a pathway to reaching a global audience that involved franchising the business. If franchising is the step that immediately precedes reaching my goal, then working backwards from this, I need to train my franchisees, have enough money to draw up a franchise agreement with an overseas lawyer, find a franchisee, and develop a franchise

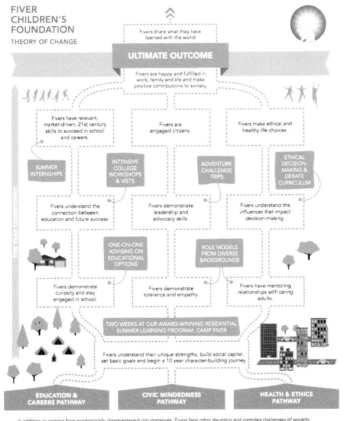

Figure 3: Example of a Theory of Change for a project working with disadvantaged children in the United States

pack that tells someone else how my business works and guarantees them a decent income for their efforts. I developed this pathway with advice from my finance director, business advisor and a lawyer, identifying missing steps and assumptions with each advisor until I had a logical pathway. In this case, the key assumption I had made until speaking to the lawyer was that drawing up a franchise agreement would be affordable, and it turned out to be well beyond my means. However, because I had traced the full pathway before embarking on it, I didn't lock my company or a franchisee into something that neither of us could afford, and I was able to create an alternative Theory of Change.

The new version in Figure 4 relies on me rather than franchisees, and aims to reach a global audience online instead. I have found that researchers often create Theories of Change that are purely about what they will do (not what they will be) to reach their goals, but it is important to remember that these are values-based goals, and this was a journey that started by identifying those priorities as they emerged at the intersection between your identity and your values. For this reason, I encourage you to explicitly identify "being" steps along the pathways you develop as part of your Theory of Change, as you can see in Figure 4. Doing this myself, I realised that there was an additional priority I was seeking, which went well beyond the father, husband, researcher and businessman I wanted to be. Like me, you may be surprised at how far you may extend your goals, as well as the clarity of pathways that emerge when you do this exercise. You can map pathways by yourself, but as I found by mapping the pathway to my goals with my business team, it is often possible to find a better path when you work with others.

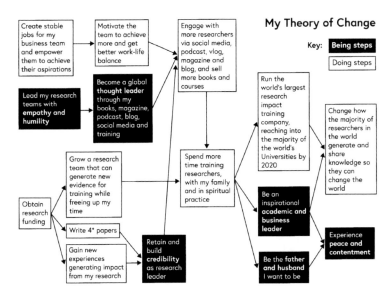

Figure 4: My Theory of Change showing what I want to do and be to reach my values-based goals

2.4 Innovate: Most techniques for managing change stop at this point, focusing on creating robust activities and pathways that will work, without leaving room for creative new thinking.

There are two approaches that I have found invaluable in stimulating innovative thinking on the pathway to your goals. The idea of "transitions management" was developed in the Netherlands to find new ways of reaching sustainable futures, and "adaptive management" came out of ecology and systems thinking, but draws on concepts from education. I have brought these approaches together in a number of my journal publications, to propose a new way of reaching goals as stretching and diverse as moving to a low carbon economy or restoring a damaged ecosystem.

The key is to turn ideas into action by experimenting with them as one of the activities or steps along the path you developed in the previous step. Rather than being afraid of the unknown, start small and learn from your mistakes. The idea of "failing fast" and "doubling your failure rate" are now commonplace in the business world in courses that teach people how to innovate to stay ahead of the competition. The fear of failure prevents people thinking big, or trying new ideas, and so they stay stuck with the familiar, which they know will work, even if it is slow and frustrating. You will already have identified things that you know will work, based on your strengths and achievements in the previous step, and they should get you to your goal in time. This final step is designed to encourage you to look around for new ways of achieving your goals that you might not previously have considered. There are three ways you can innovate as part of you plan of action:

i) Experiment: The central idea is to add "experimental" activities into the pathway you plan to reach your goals. As experiments, there is no expectation that they will necessarily work; the only expectation is that you will learn from them. As Kolb suggested in his 1984 book on *Experiential learning*, the key point is that you try things out to create concrete experiences that you can learn from, and as new ideas arise from what you learn, you try these ideas out in successive experiments that take you ever closer to your goal.

ii) Learn and adapt: The adaptive management approach provides useful advice when your experiments keep going wrong. Rather than viewing these failed experiments as mistakes, it views progress towards goals as part of an "adaptive cycle" that progresses in distinct phases. Periods of sustained growth in the natural world, as in our lives, are often followed by collapse and periods of re-organisation, in which we are forced to innovate to find new ways of working.

iii) Start small and grow: Without knowing whether or not the experiment will work, it is advisable to start small, in a safe space with people you trust, refining your ideas until you are ready to scale them up and invest real effort and resources in using these new approaches to reach your goals. Taking the analogy of the map, you may have come to realise that all the paths open to you are rocky and slow.

Instead of giving up, you stop in a wayside hut to design a vehicle that will enable you to cross the rocky paths more effectively. The first designs get stuck or break, but eventually you find something that works, and continue on your path so fast that you start overtaking everyone else, and so they then make their own versions of your vehicle, and your experimental approach becomes the norm that everyone uses.

3. How will you know it worked?

This is the final question you need to ask yourself, if you want to make systematic, measurable progress towards your goals. Many researchers I know are highly resistant to the concept of measuring progress, using things like baselines, targets and indicators. The problem, they argue, is that the metrics can end up driving us instead of the goal, and we get stuck on a linear pathway that blinkers us to shortcuts and unanticipated opportunities as they arise. Moreover, by instrumentalising success, we stop noticing the less instrumental benefits. Often, we discover that these benefits hold more value to us than the original goal, if we stop long enough to notice them.

On the other hand, I would argue that there is little point in embarking on a journey and leaving the map behind, leaving you with no way of knowing when you have reached important milestones. It is important to find out if the activities you are undertaking are actually taking you in your intended direction and helping you get closer to (not further away from) your goals. In this way, you get feedback that can empower you to correct your course, and ensure that you actually reach your goal.

Broadly speaking, there are two approaches to this: baselines and targets. For big goals, I prefer to focus on baselines from which I can measure growth and celebrate progress (no matter how small or slow), rather than fixing my attention rigidly on targets, which rarely measure up to expectations and as a result often discourage me. If you do set a target, have the humility to hold it lightly and change it if necessary, rather than punishing yourself for taking longer than you expected to reach each of your targets. When I do set myself specific targets, I try to focus on learning rather than performance targets (see the "M" of SMART in Chapter 5). For example, in my spin-out company, I measure progress from the baseline of the preceding year, celebrating each new employee, podcast download and new institution I train in as they arise. I have a target of franchising the business in the next year or so, but have conceptualised this as a series of learning tasks (as I have described in the example I gave for step 3 in Figure 2 in the previous section under "map pathways").

Having a clear sense of where we want to go and whether or not we are headed in the right direction becomes increasingly important as our careers offer us new opportunities that open up pathways to alternative destinations. In some cases, these new destinations may be better than the place we were originally headed, and it is important to keep an open mind as the journey unfolds. However, it is often difficult to see where the path leads, or to realise that saying "yes" to the next big invitation you get may actually take you off-track. The problem is that it is easier to say "yes" than it is to say "no". That's why I say "yes" to say "no", as I will explain in the next chapter.

Key lessons

- You are more likely to achieve the goals you value most. Rather than trying to change your values, understand the values that are most important to you, and find goals that arise from these values

- You may still frustrate yourself by not taking the time or the steps you know you need to take. There is a well-known gap between people's stated goals and values, and the actions they actually take. So, don't be too hard on yourself, and don't give up

- To turn your goals into action, ask what works, what will you do and how will you know it worked?

- To ask "what works", compile an evidence-base comprising: i) your own strengths, capabilities and successes; and ii) evidence of what has enabled others like you to achieve similar goals

- To ask "what will you do", visualise your goals in as precise detail as possible; make them as Stretching, Motivational, Authentic, Relational and Tailored as possible; identify activities that will enable you to reach your goal; and innovate, turning ideas into action through experimentation, learning and adaptation

- To ask "how will you know it worked", identify baselines from which you can measure growth and celebrate progress (no matter how small or slow), or set targets, with the humility to change them if necessary rather than punishing yourself for taking longer than you expected to reach them

Chapter 7
Say "yes" to say "no"

Now that you have a plan, I want to tackle the number one reason why most researchers fail to enact theirs: they become a victim of their own success. Being a researcher is endlessly fascinating, and as a career blooms, opportunities arise to do more and more cool stuff.

The more successful we become, the more important it becomes to hold onto who we are and where we fundamentally want to go. Many of the opportunities that arise may tempt us into satisfying our sense of curiosity or need for external validation, but may take us away from our values-based goals, and leave us feeling hollow as a result. As you move from being an early career researcher to a more experienced researcher, the art of retaining some semblance of work-life balance is less about what you do, and more about what you choose not to do.

Why is it so difficult to say "no"?

We may feel that we have little or no choice in the decisions we have to make. It might be in our job description to spend time doing things that take us further and further away from what we really want to do and who we really want to be. If we really do have no choice, and it is our job that is the main cause of our dissonance, then I would argue that it is time to take a long hard look at alternative careers. As an early career researcher, you may have limited choice about how you spend your time, and what you have to

89

produce. Depending on the power dynamic between you and your supervisor, this may be more or less constraining. However, whether our freedom is limited or significant, most of us have some degree of choice over the things we absolutely have to do on a day-to-day basis. For example, in some cases, we can delegate tasks to someone else who actually wants to do the thing we don't want to. Alternatively, we might find other ways of tackling the task as a team with others, to reduce the impact on us individually.

At a certain point in most research careers, there is a transition between wanting more opportunities to having too many opportunities. Sometimes this transition can be rapid, as the new opportunities you accept start to take up significant amounts of time. Very quickly, we can discover that there are too many opportunities that we don't want to miss, and too many different demands on our time.

The cumulative effect of saying "yes" to too many of these opportunities and demands, however, is usually negative. Most of us either work far longer than is good for our health or relationships to squeeze all these extra demands into our working day, or we allow the things that are most important to us (that no one else is demanding we do) to get squeezed out. As a result, we may end up spending our entire working lives fulfilling other people's dreams, while putting our own on hold.

Saying "no" sounds so easy in the cold light of day, but when strong internal motives and external incentives take you by surprise, it sometimes feels impossible to say "no" in the heat of the moment. Only much later, when the reality of the new commitment sinks in, do we realise that our failure to say "no" to the new commitment is now preventing us from doing the things that are most important to us. If only we could have had the foresight to see how much time this new commitment would take up, and what we would have to give up, it would have been so much easier to say "no" at the time.

I think there are three key reasons why is it so difficult to say "no". First, we can't help but wonder what we would be missing if we said "no". We would be saying "no" to concrete opportunities that would build our CV and might lead to other opportunities. In exchange for the self-discipline of saying "no" to these opportunities, we get the far less tangible benefits of retaining work-life balance and having time to spend on projects that are important to us. To make matters worse, this trade-off is rarely clear-cut, and we can argue to ourselves that we'll be able to squeeze in the additional work and still spend time on our other projects and get home at a decent time. Of course, logic and experience tells us that it is impossible to continue saying "yes" and have time for everything else that is important in our lives. Yet, the unrealised opportunities that lie before us continue to allure.

The second reason it is difficult to say "no" is that we feel like we are letting other people down when we refuse to help them. Sometimes colleagues may make us feel guilty if we say "no", but more frequently, we make our own choice to feel guilty. The choice to feel bad about saying "no" is predicated on the assumption that the person we decline will suffer in some way as a result our decision. This assumption may be valid in some circumstances, and we may therefore say "yes" as an act of altruism. However, this assumption is often wrong, and the negative consequences for the other person are minimal, or they are able to find what they need another way.

If you are someone who rarely asks for help, and would only ask for help if you were in desperate need and could find no other alternative, then you may assume that others are like you, and so would only ask you for help if they were in dire need. If this were true, then you would want to do anything you could to help and would probably feel guilty saying "no". On the other hand, there are many people who ask for help all the time, expecting that most people will simply say "no", and if someone does eventually agree to help it will only be because it involves little sacrifice for them. They don't feel bad asking for help because they assume other people are like them and ask for help all the time too, and will just say if they can't help. As a result, they probably say "no" themselves regularly without any feelings of guilt, and would expect you to do and feel the same. Bear this in mind, the next time someone asks you a favour. More brazen requests are not necessarily borne of adversity and may deserve more brazen answers than you are accustomed to giving.

Third, we can't help feeling privileged that we were asked. We fool ourselves into believing that we are the only person who could do the task, and take the invitation as proof that we must be the best person for the job. Some people seem to instinctively know that this is a weak point, and dress their invitations up with accolades and compliments, making it feel impossible to say "no". The reality, of course, is that if we say "no", then they will move down their list to the next person, who will probably do just as good a job as us. Ask yourself how you would feel if the person told you that they had asked someone else first and the other person had said "no". If that would change how you felt about the invitation, your feelings are probably a poor guide to making your decision. The first time this happened to me, I hadn't realised how much the invitation had inflated my ego, until I felt it deflate under the humiliation of realising that the real star of the show couldn't make it and I was the stand-in. High prestige requests often come with a lot of work, and the boosts to our CV and self-esteem are often far-off and short-lived. If our core goal is to become well known and respected by our peers, these invitations may deliver what we want. However, if our goals lie elsewhere, saying "no" to the demands of our ego is likely to deliver far greater rewards in the long term.

Say "yes" to say "no"

We have established how hard it is to say "no". It feels instinctively easier to say "yes", most of the time, and deal with the consequences later. However, if we want to stay on track to meet our goals, we have to learn how to say "no".

Or do we?

Given how easy it is to say "yes", might we be able to exploit the power of saying "yes" to our most important goals as a way of making it easier to say "no" to anything that gets in their way?

Most of us have experienced the relief of being able to get out of an unwanted invitation on the basis of an important prior commitment, in the knowledge that the person inviting us will understand and accept our reasons for declining them (for example, "my son arrives back from the other side of the world that weekend"). If the prior commitment is important to us, but we don't think the person making the invitation will understand or agree with its importance, we might feel the need to explain why ("we haven't seen him for two years"). For less important invitations, you don't even need to explain; you just say that you are busy and most people will accept your prior commitment without further comment ("sorry we'd love to but we're busy that weekend").

Now, stop and think for a moment about how you would feel if the invitation was actually someone asking you for a favour (say, house-sitting for their pets) and they demanded that you justify why you were busy, and then told you that you should really prioritise their demand. Put in blunt terms like this, it is easy to see that you are being manipulated (which I would define simply as being influenced by someone to do something for them that is against your best interests). The problem is that manipulation is rarely that easy to spot, and the demands will be dressed up with incentives, compliments and/or guilt trips.

If you have already said "yes" to spending time achieving your most important goals, and you explain to your colleagues that you have something important you have to get finished, then saying "no" will become far easier, and your colleagues will be far more likely to accept your answer. If their invitation or demand is important, but it will get in the way of you achieving goals that are important to you, then explain what you have said "yes" to, and why it is so crucial to you. If they dismiss your priorities after you have clearly articulated their importance to you, it becomes much easier to spot manipulation.

Being able to say "no" in this way requires you to have the thing you have said "yes" to at the front of your mind, ready to call to attention at a moment's notice, so you are able to evaluate whether or not the new invitation or request is compatible with achieving your goals. This is the reason I suggested you come up with a memorable and empowering word, phrase, metaphor, image or motto to sum up your identity and values as a guiding principle in Chapter 3. The idea of a guiding principle is that it is easy to call into consciousness at a moment's notice, in order to provide guidance in times of need. Simply recalling my memorable word or motto as the shortcut to my guiding principle is sometimes enough to enable me to instinctively make the right choice. Often, I need to recall the more specific values-based goal that I envisioned in Chapter 4 and then specified as a SMART goal in Chapter 5 (which is easy to do, because it follows logically from my memorable word and motto).

Recall your most Stretching, Motivational, Authentic, Relational and Tailored goal and the things you need to prioritise to reach it. Imagine yourself reaching those goals and be inspired. Say "yes" to that, and you will discover that saying "no" to everything else becomes easy.

How can it be so easy to say "no"?

Simply saying "no" may not make you many friends, but explaining why you are saying "no" can go a long way towards enabling people to accept your position. When you start saying "yes" to say "no", you will be surprised how easy it becomes to say "no", and how many people are perfectly happy to accept your reasons and find someone else to do the job.

Instead of wondering what you might miss out on if you say "no", wonder what more important things you could be displacing linked to your goals, and say "yes" to the tasks that no one is inviting you to do other than yourself, so you are motivated enough to say "no" to the commitments that might displace your goals. Instead of feeling guilty about letting other people down when you say "no", be thankful that you are not letting yourself down by chasing everyone else's dream but your own. Instead of allowing your judgement to be clouded by pride because you were invited or asked specially, strip away the emotion to see the request for what it is, and test it against your guiding principle. Only if it takes you closer to your goals is it worth agreeing. Table 2 illustrates this with examples of requests I have said "yes" or "no" to in the last three months, showing how I used my values-based goals to respond differently to seemingly similar requests.

Table 2: The last six things I said "yes" to, and last six things I said "no" to and why, showing how I used my values-based goals to respond differently to seemingly similar requests

Request	Answer	Why
Invitation to present my latest environmental research at an international conference	No	In the time I would have spent preparing for, travelling to and engaging at the conference, I can get wider readership and greater impact by creating an infographic, blog and social media strategy to promote the paper
Invitation to present my work on public and stakeholder participation to a Webinar	Yes	I am about to publish a new paper titled "a theory of participation" and want to promote its key message to researchers engaging in knowledge exchange and

hosted by a knowledge exchange network in Canada		impact. There is particular interest in impact in Canada and I want to extend my networks there
Third PhD viva request of the year	No	I said "yes" to the last two, which took far more of my time than I anticipated, and although I want to help my colleague, I want to prioritise finishing this book and the next issue of my Fast Track Impact magazine in any time I'm not doing my core job roles
Mock viva for a PhD student	Yes	Significant opportunity to help and give confidence to a philosopher studying research impact, who I can learn from
Co-Investigator on environmental research project	No	Limited potential for impact, limited funding and outputs, lots of meetings
Co-investigator on two public engagement bids	Yes	Although there is less funding and potential for research outputs than the last opportunity, there is significant potential for impact and opportunities to learn from new colleagues about how to do public engagement better
Guest editor for journal special issue	No	I feel bad saying "no" to this as the request comes from a close colleague who

		expected me to agree, but experience tells me this could suck vast amounts of time for limited benefit (it probably won't even make it onto my CV)
Co-author on a review of stakeholder engagement in species re-introductions	Yes	Opportunity to change how people in this discipline view stakeholder participation, mainstreaming the relational approach to engagement and impact at the heart of my SMART goals
Request from publisher to write a follow up to my book on climate change and land degradation	No	My co-author is now an Intergovernmental Panel on Climate Change (IPCC) author, feeding our insights directly into international policy. I don't think I can top that with a follow-up book
A book chapter in "What works in public policy"	Yes	The last edition was a best-seller for the publisher. This is an opportunity to reach new audiences with my relational approach to impact and learn from collaborators from disciplines I don't usually interact with. Based on what I learn, I can enhance my training and help more researchers engage more effectively with policymakers

Review of a grant proposal for an overseas research funder	No	Based on the abstract, it is an interdisciplinary proposal that engages stakeholders, but looks like it is just ticking boxes rather than doing anything particularly useful or inspiring. As a reviewer, there is limited potential for me to change how the team engages with stakeholders or generates impacts, and I'm not likely to learn much
Pre-review of a fellowship application for an early career colleague	Yes	It is a bit outside my field, but my experience of funding panels has the potential to make a significant difference to the success of this application. As a result of my feedback, the proposal was significantly re-written, including a much stronger pathway to impact

Of course, I'm not advocating that we all become totally self-absorbed and disregard the needs of our colleagues and students. As cooperative beings, most humans have a strong and natural urge to help others. If balanced appropriately with our own priorities, time spent in these parts of our identity can be highly rewarding. You don't have to spend the majority of your working day prioritising your own stuff, but make a habit of prioritising the things that are most important to you on a regular basis (even if that's only a few minutes of structured thinking time and note-taking per day or an hour per week writing your book). This simple act can make a significant difference to your sense of personal progress and satisfaction.

As a researcher, writing is one of the hardest tasks, in which it is tough to maintain progress and reach completion. Yet writing is an essential step for many researchers to reach their career goals. In research, your publications are your credibility, and it doesn't matter how much time you spend getting grants, invitations to speak at important events or generating impact, to get job security and have any real influence, you have to get published. In the next chapter, I want to look in more detail at the writing process, and encourage you to look critically at your current writing practice to see if you can find significant efficiencies.

Key lessons

1. As you move from being an early career researcher to a more experienced researcher, the art of retaining work-life balance is less about what you do, and more about what you choose not to do

2. We may find it hard to say "no" for fear of missing out, fear of letting others down or a desire to feel valued

3. If you have already said "yes" to spending time achieving your most important goals, and you explain to your colleagues that you have something important you have to get finished, then saying "no" will become far easier, and your colleagues will be far more likely to accept your answer

4. Recall your most Stretching, Motivational, Authentic, Relational and Tailored goal and the things you need to prioritise to reach it. Imagine yourself reaching those goals and be inspired. Say "yes" to that, and you will discover that saying "no" to everything else becomes easy

5. Don't let your newfound ability to say "no" make you selfish. Spend time helping others too. You don't have to spend the majority of your working day prioritising own stuff, but make a habit of prioritizing the things that are most important to you on a regular basis

Chapter 8

How to write a literature review in a week

Writing is a major challenge for many researchers. I will explore some of the reasons why writer's block is so prevalent and how to tackle the root causes of this problem in the next chapter. In this chapter, I want to focus on practical strategies for writing efficiently.

Don't wait for uninterrupted time to write

Before I explain my writing technique, it is worth confronting a widespread myth amongst researchers I know. This is the idea that you need to have long stretches of unbroken time if you ever want to write. Some wait years for a sabbatical, while others wait for their students to go on holiday. Most researchers are looking for at least one full, uninterrupted day. However, many tell me that this is not enough; to make real progress on a writing project, they need at least two or three uninterrupted days in a row. The problem, of course, is that this very rarely happens (even when we are on sabbatical), and as a result, writing projects are postponed indefinitely. Like many other researchers, I have now reached a stage in my career where it is challenging to find a day or more of uninterrupted writing time more than a couple of times a year. This presents us with a choice: we either adapt to our new circumstances or we stop writing.

One of the researchers I interviewed for this book, Professor Gwojen from National Taiwan University of Science and

Technology has come up with a similar approach to me to solve this problem. Instead of waiting for a "free day" to write, he breaks every writing task down into different-sized chunks. They could vary from "writing the introduction" to "write a paragraph about X" or "incorporate insights from X literature into paragraph X". Then, Professor Gwojen identifies slots of time in his schedule and matches the right-sized tasks to those slots, continuing until the last task is "proofread the full final draft".

I do most of my writing while travelling now, as my days away from home are typically full-day workshops or back-to-back meetings and my days at home tend to be punctuated by many planned calls. My busier work schedule has not prevented me from writing, as I now chunk up the writing process to fit my travel schedule. I might give myself a thinking task for the car journey to the airport, and start my literature review in the airport departure lounge, downloading key papers to read on the flight. Then during the flight I might aim to read all the papers I downloaded, or aim to write a complete first draft of the methods or results section, depending on the length of the flight. After taking a break finding the train at the other end, I might then set myself the task of reviewing what I have written so far, or looking up the papers I found in the reference lists of the papers I read on the plane, and committing to emailing the paper in whatever form it is in to my co-authors before I arrive at my destination, asking for inputs before I need to fly home again (if that's reasonable), explaining what I plan to complete on the home journey.

My writing technique

As a researcher, you have probably already developed writing techniques that work effectively for you. I am not suggesting that you necessarily adopt my technique, but as you interrogate my practice, critically examine your own practice, and see whether there are ways you might be able to significantly increase the efficiency with which you read and write for academic audiences.

I discovered this technique during my undergraduate degree when I arrived at a 9 o'clock lecture to discover my classmates handing in two essays that were due at 5 o'clock that afternoon. I had forgotten to write the deadline in my diary and hadn't started work on my essays. I was a lower second-class student at the time, but between the end of that lecture and the deadline that afternoon I produced my first ever first-class essays, scoring 90% for one and 95% for the other. I used the technique for the rest of my essays in my Undergraduate degree and Masters degree and never scored less than a first-class mark. I wrote my PhD thesis part-time with a teaching job in the same time it took many of my colleagues to write their thesis full-time. I used the technique to write my first published literature review in a week, and it has now been cited 3000 times.

I have subsequently taught my technique to hundreds of university students with an incentive to try it in practice: use my technique on any of your essays except the ones I set you, I told them, and if you don't get a first-class mark, I'll buy you a bottle of wine. In all the years I was allowed to run this scheme (I was eventually told I was making life too easy for students), only one student came to claim their bottle, but when interrogated they admitted that they had only followed half of my steps.

The principles behind my technique are basically good scholarship and efficient use of information technology to organise your thoughts:
- Learn how to speed-read: you don't need to read every word of every paper you cite
- Stay focused on your question(s) so you can extract the key points
- Organise what you've read efficiently
- Find a system to link key points together into critical arguments as part of an overall narrative
- Put clear limits on the number of hours you work if you want to retain a creative edge

Table 3 shows what my week might look like if I'm writing a literature review from scratch. I have designed this for writing a literature review for submission to a journal, which might be anywhere between 5,000-8,000 words long. You can follow the same process, but expand it to five weeks rather than five days for a book-writing project. Finally, many of the papers and books we will write as researchers have many other components in addition to a literature review. This process applies to the literature review component of that project, and therefore it may take you significantly less than a week to complete.

Table 3: How to write a literature review in a week

Day and time	Task
Day 1: Scoping your search terms and general reading	
09.00-10.00	Scoping
10.00-17.00	General reading
Day 2: Concept mapping and targeted reading	
09.00-11.00	Concept mapping
11.00-14.00	Thinking time
14.00-17.00	Targeted reading
Day 3: Targeted reading and writing your introduction	
09.00-12.00	Draft your introduction
13.00-17.00	Targeted reading
Day 4: Write your first full draft	
09.00-17.00	Writing
Day 5: Review your draft and finalise your work	
09.00-17.00	Reviewing and writing

Day 1: Scoping your search terms and general reading

09.00-10.00 Scoping:
- Do an internet search to refine your search terms, using a standard search engine like Google, browsing widely to get a sense of the different ways people are writing about your topic area. I may have started with a fairly narrow remit, constrained through my use of language to a single discipline or tradition, but now I am aware of other terms being used in different disciplines or other contexts, and related concepts. One of the most challenging criticisms from reviewers is that you missed an important search term that would have completely changed the outcome of your review had you included it. This first step reduces the likelihood of becoming blinkered by your disciplinary roots.
- Drawing on as many of your search terms as possible, create an overarching question that your reading will answer. If necessary, you can break this down into a set of related sub-questions, but try and keep this to the bare minimum, so it is easy to keep your question in mind at all times. Write this question and your search terms on a piece of paper and stick it to your wall or computer, and keep it at the forefront of your mind for the whole process

10.00-17.00 General reading:
- Prioritise what you read by relevance, making sure the scholarly search engine you use is set to sort results by relevance rather than date. If you use Google Scholar, it will also prioritise by citations, so you may need to follow up with a search of material published in the last 2–3 years, which may be highly relevant but has not yet attracted many citations.
- Speed-read the search results:
  - Keeping your overarching question(s) and search terms clearly in your mind, quickly read the titles of the articles and books that come up in your search, skipping to the next title as soon as it becomes

clear that a title isn't relevant (you might only read the first three words of the title to determine that it is not relevant). Only read the full title if you think it might be relevant
- o If (and only if) you think the title looks relevant, move to the abstract. Read the first one or two sentences and the last sentence to quickly determine if it is actually relevant, and only if it is relevant, read the full abstract
- o If the abstract has only minor or tangential relevance, make a note of the point you think might be relevant and go back to your search
- o Only if the abstract suggests the publication is highly relevant to your question do you then access the publication
- o Remain sceptical as to the relevance of the publication, and start by reading the introduction and conclusion to confirm its relevance. If it is genuinely relevant, read the full paper. If you're not sure how relevant it is, save it to come back to later, and don't waste time reading it now
- o Instantly, you have significantly reduced the number of words you have to read, saving you time, and reducing the likelihood that you go off at tangents from your topic. The key to this working is being highly disciplined in your focus, returning to your questions(s) and keywords as soon as you lose sight of them and start going down an interesting but potentially less relevant side street
- Create a searchable system for thematically organising what you learn from your reading. I use a spreadsheet for this task:
  - o I copy and paste relevant sentences/paragraphs to cells in Column A, putting them into themes that help answer my question as I go
  - o In column B, I paraphrase what the quote means in relation to my question in as few words as possible
  - o In column C, I copy and paste the full reference (by hitting the "cite" link on Google Scholar) so it is

easy to compile my reference list later. If you're using citation management software, put it in there too for later

- As I read new material that adds to a theme, I insert rows in my spreadsheet and put the material under the relevant theme. Sometimes, it becomes clear that there are a number of sub-themes emerging within a theme, and so I pull out those sub-themes, using a numbering or formatting system to show that they relate to a higher-level theme. Sometimes the opposite happens, and I realise that writers from two different disciplines are actually talking about the same thing using different words, and I merge two themes into one
- I stop reading at 5 o'clock and take the evening off, even if it feels like I've only scratched the surface. This is important because at this point, many people continue reading without realizing that they have fallen into a narrow or partial reading of their question. The next step is designed to identify if this has happened and help you broaden your reading to cover the relevant breadth of material efficiently

Day 2: Concept mapping and targeted reading

09.00-11.00 Concept mapping:
- After a good night's sleep, I review the previous day's work, focusing on the themes that emerged from my reading. I resist the temptation to continue reading at this point
  - Sort the themes and sub-themes into a coherent structure. Which themes come first, and which come later? Which themes are linked to each other and how? I like to use a mind-map for this, using as few words as possible. You could create a more standard spider diagram, on the wall with Post-it™ notes or on a whiteboard. Alternatively, you could just copy and paste the themes and sub-themes from your spreadsheet into a word processing document, and play with their order using bullets

and sub-bullets or numbered lists, till you are happy that you have found a coherent structure that links your themes
- o Look for the most important themes that provide the most powerful or useful answers to your question, and see if you can aggregate your themes under the smallest possible number of meta-themes. These meta-themes will provide a strong overall structure to your argument, and may end up forming sub-titles in your written work
- o Now look for gaps. These may be apparent just by looking at the density of branches in your mind-map or sub-bullets in your word-processed list of themes. Which elements have least detail, and do you think this lack of detail might represent a gap in your knowledge of the subject? Another approach is to look for additional links. Which themes do you think should in theory be linked in some way, and have you read anything that would suggest a link? If not, might this represent a gap in your knowledge?

11.00-14.00 Thinking time:
- Go for a walk, take lunch with a friend, forget about work
- Let your review structure gradually settle in your mind
- Try and get some distance from your work, so you can come back and see a bird's eye view of the whole narrative as it is forming, to check if it really holds together coherently
- Alter your structure and look for additional gaps

14.00-17.00 Targeted reading:
- Do targeted literature searches to plug gaps in your knowledge, based on the concept mapping you have done
- Integrate what you learn into your spreadsheet under each of the emergent themes
- Stop reading at 5 o'clock, no matter how fascinating it is or how much more you now realise you need to read.

Don't worry, you can pick this up again in the morning, and you'll be faster and more focused after a good night's sleep

Day 3: Targeted reading and writing your introduction

09.00-12.00: Draft your introduction:
- Although you haven't finished reading yet, now is the time to write the hardest part of your literature review, when you've read enough to get a sense of the key arguments and the structure you will follow, and while you are still fresh. Don't put this off. Give yourself a strict deadline before lunch to have a rough draft of your introduction, including clear aims, and put pen to paper.
- This step is an additional check to make sure that the structure you developed yesterday really does work, and that there aren't any major gaps in your logic or planned structure. Sometimes this only becomes apparent when we try and write the introduction

13.00-17.00 Targeted reading:
- After rewarding yourself with a good lunch break, continue with your targeted reading, adapting what you read to any gaps you identified while writing your introduction
- Return to any of the most relevant papers you didn't have time to read properly on the first day and read them in detail

Day 4: Write your first full draft

Now you need to actually write your literature review. Two days is more than enough if you have followed the preceding steps, because now you have a detailed blueprint for your review:
- Follow the structure you have laid out in your mind-map, cross-referencing from each branch of the mind-map to the relevant theme heading in your spreadsheet

- Read through your paraphrases (column B) to get a sense of what the literature says about a particular theme, and start to arrange this in your mind into a coherent structure, swapping the order or rows around in the spreadsheet to help you remember how the argument is forming in your mind
- Write a paragraph or sub-section based on the material in that theme, copying and pasting your original paraphrasing into your review if you get stuck, and referencing the relevant literature for each point you pull out of the spreadsheet

Day 5: Review your draft and finalise your work

Even if you didn't finish a full draft yesterday, start your last day by reviewing what you've written so far, refining your language and arguments. Finish the remaining sections and send to a friendly colleague for pre-review feedback or co-authorship. This may throw up a few additional jobs you have to complete before you can finalise your manuscript for submission, but you will have broken the back of this task in a week, and it will feel like you're cycling downhill from here.

What will you do differently?

As I said at the start of this chapter, few researchers will want to adopt my technique exactly as I use it. My hope instead is that you look at this technique and ask yourself if there might be ways of adapting your own writing process to become significantly more efficient. How focused are you when you write? Do you prioritise resting and thinking time, as well as time for reading and writing? How efficient are your methods of identifying and linking relevant points from the literature? Can you find more efficient ways of identifying and structuring arguments that make it quicker and easier to write well?

There are two reasons why my technique saves time, and these can be generalised to apply to your own writing technique. The first is that I am reading fewer words. A number of the techniques I use are designed to reduce the number of words I have to read, from speed-reading selected parts of the publications I identify as relevant, to identifying key insights and structure as I read, so I can identify gaps and prioritise my searching and reading to fill those gaps instead of reading endlessly until something coherent emerges. I know when to stop reading because I reach a point at which there are increasingly fewer new ideas emerging from what I have read; I have reached "theoretical saturation". The second reason that my technique saves time is that I have a method (based loosely on Grounded Theory Analysis) for identifying emergent themes, which helps me structure my thinking, and hence my writing, providing me with a road map to the eventual paper, section by section, paragraph by paragraph, which when complete retains a critical and coherent overarching narrative.

What methods do you use to get through the volume of reading that is necessary for a good literature review, how do you decide when to stop reading, and how do you keep track of the themes and insights that emerge as you read? If you do not already have answers to these questions, I hope that my technique might inspire you to develop some new methods of your own which will provide you with the answers.

If the secret to writing fast is reading less, then what else might we be able to do more efficiently if we thought differently about the way we use our time? In the next chapter, I want to broaden the idea of "doing less to do more" to encompass the full range of tasks we are likely to encounter as a researcher, and show the vital importance of rest and work-life balance if we want to stay productive and fulfilled.

Key lessons

1. Don't wait for uninterrupted time to write. Instead, break every writing task down into different-sized chunks and identify slots in your schedule and match the right-sized tasks to these slots

2. Learn how to speed-read: you don't need to read every word of every paper you cite

3. Stay focused on your question(s) so you can extract the key points

4. Organise what you've read efficiently

5. Find a system to link key points together into critical arguments as part of an overall narrative

6. Put clear limits on the number of hours you work if you want to retain a creative edge

Chapter 9
Do less to do more

I am often surprised at how long a simple task can take. Often, however, the problem lies not with the task, but with the amount of time I allow it to consume. Tasks have a habit of swelling to fill the time you give them. If I give myself a month to write a literature review, I scatter writing slots across my diary, reading for as long as I can, before eventually committing pen to paper and still end up short of time as the deadline approaches. I used to give myself a day to prepare a lecture, and it would always take at least a day, often spilling into the morning of the lecture.

"Good enough"

Tasks have a habit of fitting the time we give them, if we have a rigid deadline. I often end up finishing my meeting preparation, or completing the slides for my talk, just as the train is drawing into the station. This timing is no co-incidence. I made the task fit the time I had available on the train, and discovered that I had read *enough* of the papers for the meeting, and my slides were *good enough*.

Could I have read more and have been better prepared? Yes. Would it have significantly improved my performance at the meeting? Probably not, but it would have displaced something else that as a result would not have been done. Could my slides have been better? Yes, I would have added in some powerful images, converted bullet points on slides into notes that I would have printed out, and I might even have memorised parts of the talk and rehearsed it. In this case, it could have significantly improved my performance, but would that have really mattered? Again, probably not. In fact, if I speak for less time, it allows more time for questions, and most of the audience learn more from the discussion than they would have done from an additional five minutes of content.

Recently I *almost* got away with preparing a plenary talk from scratch while the speakers before me were presenting. In this case, I had not planned to be so under-prepared. I had completely forgotten that I was meant to be speaking. I arrived at the venue five minutes before the first session began, and noticed my name on the list of speakers as I was walking into the auditorium. I hurriedly found the organiser and told them that I didn't have my talk on a stick and would be using my own laptop to show my slides. That gave me time to sit at the back with my laptop and construct my slides. I had time to construct six slides before my time was up. As a result, I had very little material on the screen, but this helped me zoom out to give a big picture overview of the core things I thought were most important. I delivered what I had to say in the time allotted with more passion than most of the previous speakers, possibly fuelled by my nerves. I was the last person on before the break, and after the organiser closed the session, she came up to me and thanked me for my talk. I confessed that I'd been delayed in travel the night before, and had slept in, and only realise I was speaking when I arrived in the room. As I was speaking, one of the delegates shouted over to me to say that my radio microphone was still hooked up and everyone was listening in to our conversation. I almost got away with it, but not quite.

Taking a "good enough" approach requires you to assess exactly what will be "good enough". This recognises that a "good enough" performance in one context, for one purpose, may not be good enough in another context, for another purpose. Sometimes the stakes are too high, and there is no option but to prepare thoroughly. As such, there shouldn't be such a thing as "good enough" data analysis (although ongoing debate about the role of "p values" in science might make you wonder). A talk that is good enough for a departmental seminar may not be good enough for an invited talk to the United Nations.

I have never prepared more than I did for a talk I was invited to give recently to a United Nations conference in Mexico. It turned out to be the toughest presentation of my life, and literally almost killed me. They had commissioned me and a colleague to write a report, and in the small print our contract stated that we would deliver a presentation about the report at the Mexico conference. The problem was that it fell at a particularly challenging time for my family, when my wife was working away from home, and it would have created major childcare issues. So I explained that my co-author would be in Mexico for the conference and she could deliver the talk. But no, they wanted me to do it. I told them I could deliver it via video link; it was about climate change after all, so maybe it would be a good thing not to fly all the way to Mexico to deliver my talk? But no, they wanted me in person. I explained that I had childcare issues, which meant that I couldn't leave till the Monday and would have to be back on the Tuesday, which clearly wasn't possible. They booked me a return flight.

I realise that I would need to be at my best, so I found an inspiring story from one of the people I had interviewed in the Kalahari Desert a few years previously as a hook for my talk, made slides with images and key words, and committed the whole thing to memory. I commissioned a film-maker to create an animation to illustrate my take-home point, and created a rousing speech at the end which scrolled up the screen, line by line, as I spoke. The speech was meant to make people sit up and listen because it appeared to be saying the exact opposite of everything you would expect me to say in conclusion. Then the scrolling text on the screen stopped, and started scrolling in the opposite direction, and I read the same speech, line by line, but in reverse order, and I delivered the rousing conclusion that they were expecting, in line with our research findings.

There was just one problem. I suffer from asthma, and was recovering from a chest infection. As I was briefing the interpreters at the back of the hall before I went on, I realise that I was beginning to have an asthma attack. I also realise that I was sweating profusely, but not from nerves. As I took medication to get the asthma under control, I realise that I was shaking uncontrollably with a fever, and my legs started to buckle beneath me. My collaborator helped me find a steward, who told me that they had a doctor on site. I showed the doctor my asthma medication, which included some fairly high dose steroids at the time, and she decided to give me a high dose steroid injection.

The result was quite remarkable. Within minutes, the shaking had stopped and I was able to get to my feet again. I was rushed back to the auditorium where various dignitaries were opening the event. I arrived as I was about to be introduced. The chair started, "I am sorry to announce that...", and then paused. Someone had approached him from behind and was whispering something in his ear. "...Professor Mark Reed will now address us", he continued. As I stood on that stage, still drenched in sweat, I was extremely thankful that I had prepared as well as I had. The presentation went perfectly, and then I was bundled into a taxi back to the airport.

I started this story by telling you that this talk almost killed me. Well, the doctor had given me tablets and told me the precise time I needed to take them, halfway across the Atlantic. I took them and felt progressively more ill. I sat in one position, awake for the whole flight, and had actually worn a hole in the elbows of my suit jacket by the time we landed. When I went to my doctor the next day, the first thing she did was to confiscate the steroid vials I had been given as they were apparently not legal in my home country. She then looked at the tablets I had been given to take in the air, and explained that the doctor's plan must have been to step me down slowly from the massive dose of steroids I'd been given, but the tablets she had given me were anti-histamines with such a small dose of steroid in them that my dosage had effectively fallen off a cliff halfway

120

across the Atlantic. Apparently, I was lucky I hadn't had a heart attack.

The point I am trying to make with my "presentation from hell" story is that sometimes it is worth preparing a lot. However, you usually know which things you need to prepare for, and most things do not require a level of preparation or effort anywhere close to what I put into that talk. I've spoken about presentations that are good enough, but might it be possible to extend this to writing that is good enough?

What if I only gave myself a week to write my next literature review? Would the result be good enough? The literature review might not be good enough to be published, but it would be good enough to send to co-authors, and actually not that far off being publishable. In case you are wondering, these are exactly the kind of deadlines I often set myself, and the results are good enough by most people's standards. Since I finished by PhD 12 years ago, I've published an average of eight papers per year in top journals and so far they've amassed over 10,000 citations, suggesting that others find them useful.

The key lesson I have learned is to limit the time I give to the tasks I need to do. The strange thing is that the end product is usually as good, and sometimes actually better, than if I had spent double the time on the task. I believe that the reason for this is that the level of focused attention provided by a forced deadline actually enables me to produce more focused work, compared to fracturing that work over a longer period of less focused time.

Work less to write more

If "do less to do more" works as a general principle, for the reasons I have suggested at the end of the last section, I would like to apply that principle to writing in this section. I have learned to set myself strict limits on how much time I will commit to writing on any given project. As a result, I may not have read everything that has ever been written on the topic before committing pen to paper, but the chances are that Google Scholar has identified the most important things for me to read, based on relevance to my key words and citations, and I'll do a specific search for articles published in the last two or three years that may not have gained many citations yet, but that are highly relevant to my work.

This is not fool-proof, but I trust that my co-authors or pre-review feedback will bring up anything important that I might have missed. Sending the product of a day's work (if that's all the time I could allocate to the task) to co-authors, with the necessary caveats of "rough draft" and "work in progress", takes some nerve. What if I missed something really obvious? If I did, then I have two options: to feel embarrassed or to learn from my colleagues. If you want to write collaboratively, you have to be willing to accept that you might be wrong and to be able to deal with the consequences of interacting with colleagues who disagree with what you have written. If you wait until your work is perfect because you cannot cope with negative feedback, you may never send your work to colleagues, and if you do, you may resent every sentence they delete or change, making it difficult to learn from your co-author's perspectives or work collaboratively together.

Taking a "good enough" approach to writing is unlikely to get you published in the top journals and, depending on your subject area, may be disastrous if "good enough" turns out to be factually inaccurate. The strength of the "good enough" approach to writing is that it forces you to collaborate with others, who in turn may reciprocate by giving you opportunities to collaborate with them. While this works most effectively in disciplines where there is a culture of multi-authored outputs, it can also work well for dual-author teams. Indeed, although most of my papers have multiple authors, much of this output has been split mainly with one other author, with smaller inputs from others to plug gaps or to acknowledge their role in collecting and analysing data.

These informal "writing circles" can be incredibly productive. The basic idea is that a group of authors band together to write a series of papers, taking it in turn to be lead author. In a group of four researchers, each researcher only has to lead the production of one paper, with smaller inputs to the other papers, but they get four papers out of the collaboration.

My most productive writing circle was with a team of 20 researchers as part of a research project. We established a group norm that anyone in the group would send a concept note to the group describing their next paper from the project. Anyone from the group could then propose a contribution they would like to make to the paper, and the lead author would decide whether or not they thought the contribution would add value to the paper. The result was that many papers took new directions that the lead author would have never pursued had they worked alone or only with the team from their Work Package, and the interdisciplinary nature of the papers meant that they appealed to wider audiences, attracting more citations. By the end of the project, we had published over 50 papers in top journals as a team. As a result, each of the post-doctoral researchers on the project are now either associate professors or full professors. You don't have to be invited to join a writing circle – you can create one of your own. I've explained how in Box 4.

The number one reason good researchers don't get published is that they don't submit their work for publication, waiting instead until it is as perfect as possible, or worse still, listening to the imaginary voices of the reviewers and editors who rubbish each sentence as they write it. There are many sources of "writer's block", but the most common I have encountered is lack of confidence. This lack of confidence prevents researchers reaching out to colleagues to collaborate, making it impossible to form a writing circle or get pre-review feedback to help smooth the publication process. If you lack confidence, it is difficult to collaborate with others because you are forced to share incomplete or rough drafts with others who will point out your ill-formed ideas and mistakes. Even worse than this, if you do get a scathing rejection from the journal, all of your co-authors will receive your feedback and as lead author the shame will fall on you. If these issues plague your writing, go back and take a long hard look at the material in Chapters 2 and 3 of this book. It is likely that you will have tried every writing and time management technique available, but breaking through your writer's block is likely to be a deeper work.

Box 4: How to form a high-performing writing circle

There are two ways you can form a writing circle. The formal approach is typically planned and organised by a group of researchers who share similar interests and have complementary expertise:

- Identify researchers with similar interests and complementary expertise, who each have the ability to successfully lead papers for publication in good journals

- Establish the ground rules, for example:
  - o All papers from a joint project may be offered for co-authorship to all other team members, with the lead author retaining the power to veto a contribution they do not feel would add value to the paper

  - o Each member of the writing circle commits to offer co-authorship to the other members of the group on at least one paper that year (publication outlines may be exchanged at the outset to draft a publication schedule for the group), and each member commits to make a substantive contribution to the papers they are invited to join (this may already be identified as part of the scoping exercise of drafting paper outlines)

Alternatively, you can create a writing circle informally with almost anyone, but there are no guarantees that your offers of co-authorship will be reciprocated using this method:

- For this to work, you have to have a credible enough track record as a researcher, for other researchers to believe that if they co-author with you, they will actually get a publication out of the process

- Reach out to prolific researchers who have a track record of leading multi-authored papers in good journals, and may be more likely to accept your invitation and have the capacity to reciprocate if they wish in future

- Offer co-authorship in return for a substantive contribution that adds value (this means you are not committed to accepting the contribution if you do not see it as substantive or useful) to a paper that would benefit from additional sections or insights, which you request from co-authors with relevant expertise

- If nothing else, these prolific researchers will engage deeply enough with your work via the co-authorship process that they are more likely than before to cite the paper they write with you and your previous work. As you consistently offer opportunities for collaboration, leading to successful publication, these researchers learn more about your expertise and are more likely to reach out to you the next time they need the expertise you hold

Work harder at resting

Finally, the most important lesson from my "do less to do more" principle applies to the working day. Where do you draw the line and decide to stop working? The tasks of a researcher do not stop at 5 o'clock on a Friday afternoon. We cannot hand over our patients to the night-shift team and go home to our beds, because we *are* the team. If we don't do the job, it won't get done. Yet, we do draw that line somewhere, and I would argue that the place we draw the line is largely arbitrary. No matter how late we work, when we decide to stop there is always more we could or should have done. We draw that line, and the tasks that are outstanding get postponed or are never completed.

The insight we need is to realise that we will never get everything done. It wouldn't matter if we were able to work 24 hours a day; there would still be tasks outstanding. The reason for this, as I explained at the start of this chapter, is that tasks swell to fill the time we give them. This doesn't only apply to the length of time an individual task takes. It also applies to the number of tasks that we are given or take on. If I decide to work 50% more hours than my colleague, I will probably find 50% more things to say "yes" to, and people will increasingly gravitate to me with their requests. If we draw our line at a place where we do 50% fewer hours than our colleagues, we may discover that we do not produce significantly less, and by following the advice in this book, we may in fact produce more. I probably work fewer hours than the average academic, but there is no evidence that I am any less productive.

In fact, there is evidence that people typically become more productive when they work shorter hours. A study of World War 1 munitions workers by John Pencavel in *The Economic Journal* in 2015 showed how workers who worked more than 50 hours a week became no more productive, with those working 72 hours per week producing no more than their counterparts who worked 12 hours less (see how the weekly output levels off after 50 hours in Figure 5). OECD figures tell a similar story, showing a negative correlation between the number of hours worked per person and the Gross Domestic Product that is produced per hour of work. Countries where people worked the least number of hours had the highest productivity per hour of work.

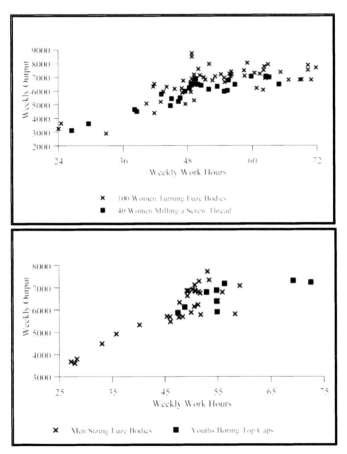

Figure 5: Weekly output of munitions based on the weekly hours of 100 women turning fuze bodies, 40 women milling a screw thread, 56 men sizing fuze bodies and 15 youths boring top caps (from Pencavel J. 2015. The productivity of working hours. *The Economic Journal 125*: 2052-2076)

Working long hours isn't just bad for productivity; it is bad for your health. A meta-analysis of 21 studies published in the *Journal of Occupational and Organisational Psychology* in 1997 by Kate Sparks and colleagues showed a small but significant correlation between the number of hours worked and physiological and psychological health symptoms. A more recent systematic review published in 2015 by Akira Bannai and Akiko Tamakoshi in the *Scandinavian Journal of Work, Environment & Health* concluded that working long hours was associated with depression, anxiety, sleep conditions and coronary heart disease.

Writing in his 1897 book, *Advice for a Young Investigator*, neurobiologist Santiago Ramón y Cajal complained that "research is now frantic" and argued that the pursuit of productivity would promote superficial enquiry compared to the insights he argued were more likely to emerge from the "silence of study", concentrating "for extended periods of time on one subject" and "tranquil meditations". More recently, Nassim Nicholas Taleb wrote in his 2010 book, *The Bed of Procrustes: Philosophical and Practical Aphorisms*, "Only in recent history has working hard signalled pride rather than shame". I do not interpret these admonitions to mean we should avoid work, or that hard work is necessarily unhealthy. As Alex Soojung-Kim Pang put it in his 2016 book, *Rest: why you get more done when you work less*, "Rest is not work's adversary. Rest is work's partner. They complement and complete each other. You cannot work well without resting well."

If you are serious about becoming more productive, you need to become serious about resting well. Only by taking it seriously are you likely to prioritise it enough to make time for it, especially when making time for rest means you have to say "no" to an opportunity or get an extension to a deadline. By "resting well" I mean far more than just getting enough sleep or being idle. I am talking about active rest that deeply refreshes, inspires and energises us. Instead of watching TV, get some exercise or engage in something creative or imaginative like fixing or making something, gardening or reading a book. Instead of napping or getting drunk, try meditating or engaging in some other spiritual practice. Ramón y Cajal advised us that if our research does not yield useful findings, "yet we feel success is just around the corner, try resting for a while … relaxation and quiet in the countryside brings calmness and clarity to the mind" and "intellectual refreshment". If you are going to watch TV, find something that will expand your mind or inspire you rather than just watching whatever is on at the time, and if you are going to get drunk, do it with old friends. These sorts of activities re-energise us because they help diffuse stress and clear the mind, connecting us to our values and identity, and our fundamental motivations. As a result, we return to work sharper, more focused and more motivated.

Taking deliberate, high-quality rest is a skill. You need to do it "on purpose" and you need to practice if you want to get better at it. The irony is that you may feel too tired to rest properly, but breaking poor rest habits can yield benefits in terms of the peace of mind and motivation that reward new habits quickly. The pay-back can be particularly rewarding for academics, who often struggle to "see the wood for the trees", given the complexity of the work we do. As we rest, research findings and other ideas have time and space to settle in our minds, and we start to see the big picture insights that have been alluding us. This explains why some of our greatest ideas occur to us when we are in the shower or on a walk. In fact, the last time I had a "eureka moment" was during a duathlon. As a result of the idea that struck me at that moment, I missed a large luminous green arrow and got lost. I only realise my mistake when I reached the end of the road, knocked on the door of the farmhouse I found there, and was told that there was a turning a few miles back down the road. I came last in the race, but had won a far more important academic prize.

In *A Room of One's Own*, Virginia Woolf compares the lives of male academics in well-funded, ancient colleges to the more frugal academic life at newer women's colleges. She argued that the ancient colleges offered far more opportunities for success, not as a direct result of their greater riches, but because their research budgets gave faculty members time for long walks and lengthy conversations. Similarly, James Watson's account of his and Francis Crick's discovery of the structure of DNA includes descriptions of long lunches at the Eagle pub, afternoon walks around Cambridge, time spent browsing in book shops, playing tennis or visiting the Alps. Making time to rest isn't just good for your mental and physical health; it is good for your intellect and creativity. That's why getting work-life balance is so important, and that is why the messages in this book are so crucial for researchers to understand.

What will you cut?

For the average over-committed researcher, making room to rest requires a bit of pruning. In this conclusion to the chapter, I want you to make a list of all the things you could cut back which could make room for your most important priorities, and make time for genuine rest a real possibility.

Think back to the last three things you did in your last three months of work that gave you a real sense of satisfaction. What proportion of the last three months did you spend directly working on the tasks that gave you so much satisfaction? Although answers can vary substantially, most people when asked this question would say that they only spent a minority of their time directly working on these tasks. This raises an important question. What were you doing with the rest of your time that did not result in outcomes that you value?

If you had a clearer sense of your goals, do you think it would be easier to spend more time focused on tasks that directly contribute towards achieving them, and reduce the amount of time you spend on everything else? If you spent even a small fraction of every day (or at least every week) dedicated to directly working on your most important goals, do you think you might make steadier progress towards reaching your goals? How do you think this would impact on your motivation?

I have worked with many people who tell me that this one simple action is transformational: spend time every day or week working directly on your most important goals. Even if you only spend ten minutes, the impact of making incremental but regular progress can transform your levels of motivation, and help you become significantly more focused. The more rewards you get from the small amount of time you invest in this approach, the more incentive you have to increase that time, and further prioritise your goals. It becomes self-reinforcing.

You could get up earlier in the morning to spend an hour writing (or doing whatever that important task is). I've never been motivated enough to do that consistently, but the point I'm trying to make is that you don't have to spend all day doing the important stuff, but you do have to keep chipping away at it. The more focused you become on your goals, the easier it becomes to say "no" and the more likely your colleagues are to accept your answer because they understand the importance of the things you have already said "yes" to. Do less to do more. Limit your tasks to only the most important, so that you shorten the amount of time you have to work. Then, shorten the amount of time you have to work, so that you are forced to limit your tasks to only the most important.

Key lessons

1. The problem with a task that takes longer than expected, lies not with the task, but with the amount of time you allow the task to consume

2. When you limit the time you give to a task within reason, the end product is often as good, if not better, than if you had allowed the task to swallow double the time. The level of focused attention provided by a forced deadline can enable more focused and therefore better work

3. Many good researchers don't get published because they don't submit their work for review, waiting instead until it is perfect, or worse still, give themselves "writer's block" by listening to the imaginary voices of reviewers who rubbish each sentence as they write it

4. This lack of confidence prevents researchers reaching out to colleagues to collaborate, making it impossible to form a writing circle or get pre-review feedback to help smooth the publication process

5. Where we draw the line between work and home is largely arbitrary. There will always be unfinished tasks on our to-do list, no matter how late we work

6. If you worked for 50% less time than your colleagues, and that forced you to prioritise better, you would not be 50% less productive. In fact, hour-on-hour, you would probably be more productive

7. You cannot work well without resting well. If you are serious about becoming more productive, you need to become serious about resting well

8. Spend time every day or week working directly on your most important goals. Even if you only spend 10 minutes, the impact of making incremental but regular progress can transform your levels of motivation, and help you become significantly more focused

Chapter 10
How to spend less time on emails and meetings

Whether your goal is to write a literature review or something else, there are two things that in my experience are most likely to get in the way of you achieving your goals as a researcher: endless emails and meetings. In this chapter, I want to show how you can put the principles from the first part of this book into practice at key pinch points in your working day, to stay focused on your goals. There are no simple answers – daily life as a researcher is a balancing act between prioritising your goals and being a responsible member of the research community who helps others. For each of the issues, I have explained how I have personally applied the principles in Part 1 to find a balance I am content with. I invite you to ask yourself some hard questions about how you deal with these challenges in your day-to-day work, and find answers that are appropriate for you.

The tyranny of email

There is something mildly tyrannical about email. If you feel compelled to check your email in the middle of an important task, there is a good chance that you are not simply motivated by the reward of what might be waiting for you, but rather by some kind of fear of what might be lurking there that needs to be dealt with. I think a lot of us have some kind of blind, unreasoned fear that something bad will happen if we do not reply to an important email before the end of the day. Depending on how important or scary the email is, I feel a very real pressure to reply immediately. The only negative consequence is the unease I feel until I've replied, and the impact of my response on what I was actually meant to be doing that morning. If I wait a day, there is rarely any major fall-out, and my response is likely to be more considered and not interrupt my workflow. The tyranny of email is very real, but it is entirely self-made. I allow it to dominate me because I am worried about what people will think of me if I don't respond to their demands in time.

The only way to break the tyranny of email is to understand the negative feelings it gives voice to. Stop comparing the number of emails you had when you returned from holiday with your colleagues to establish that you really do have a bigger challenge than everyone else. Instead, realise that everyone in that conversation, including the new member of staff who received half the volume of emails, probably feels the same pressure. I have certainly heard junior colleagues complaining about volumes of email I could only dream of, and yet they feel just as much pressure from these few emails as I do from many more. It is clear to me that the problem is not the volume of emails we receive, but how we perceive them.

Without dealing with our perception of email, none of the techniques for getting on top of your email will work (such as the "one touch principle", where you act on, file or delete each email the first time you open it, without leaving and returning to it later). Your emails will remain on top of you, as long as you continue giving them psychological power. A favourite technique among some of my colleagues at the moment is the "zero inbox" approach where you make sure you clear your inbox, dealing with every query, on a daily basis. This works because it clears that sense of guilt or impending doom that hangs over you, not knowing what is in your inbox, or putting off dealing with difficult queries. However, for me, this technique makes email more tyrannical than ever before; we appease our guilt by feeding the email monster with our most precious commodity, time. With the volume of emails many researchers get, to achieve a "zero inbox" every day would require a very significant proportion of the day, and significantly reduce the time left for prioritising the most important tasks.

Email, and the urgent tasks it brings, is probably the number one distraction that prevents researchers from achieving their goals. The key insight is to recognise the magnitude of email's insidious threat, and then to try and get some perspective on the demands it brings you each day. If you were to stop and think about the urgency and importance of each of the things you've been asked to do via email, and compare these to the importance of your most crucial goals, would you make an explicit trade-off and compromise goals to keep everyone in your inbox happy? In some cases, there will be things that are genuinely urgent, and have to take priority. However, this is rarely the case. Ruthlessly prioritising, like the people I interviewed in Chapter 3 do, requires you to be more ruthless about the extent to which you allow email to take you away from your prime focus. Saying "yes" to say "no" to your email means focusing on the things that are most important to you every day, so you can immediately recognise when tasks from your email are going to compromise the important goals you have said "yes" to. Then, focusing on the goals you have said "yes" to, you can explain politely that you can't help on this occasion or that the person will have to wait a bit longer than they might want.

I sometimes have bad days where I allow my email to dominate, and finish the day feeling as though I have worked hard but achieved nothing. On a good day, however, I do a scan of the most important and urgent emails in the morning and only reply to these, ignoring the rest till the afternoon, often after lunch when I'm feeling most tired and less able to give quality attention to my most important work. If necessary, I will send a holding email, acknowledging the email and explaining that I've got a busy morning and that I'll reply later in the day. Often I will ask when an important task needs to be done at the latest, and forward the email to my to-do list with a deadline (I use Evernote to do this without leaving my email programme, sending the email to my unique Evernote email address, and then adding it to my Evernote shortcuts, which is where I keep my to-do list). If I've got a writing deadline (even if it's self-imposed), I will put an out-of-office reply up, explaining that I'm working towards an important deadline and not checking emails for the rest of the week, and to send me a text message if it is urgent.

These are just examples of how I personally try to implement what I'm suggesting. The practical techniques are not important. What is important is that you understand why you give email the power to distract and divert you. If you can make these reasons explicit in your mind, you may be able to look more objectively at the urgency and importance of the tasks that arrive via email, and compare them to the urgency and importance of the goals you are trying to focus on. The more you make this more objective comparison and say "no" to or at least delay tasks so they don't compromise your goals, the more likely it is that you will overcome the tyranny of email.

How many reviews are enough?

One of the most frequent requests many researchers will receive via email (on an almost daily basis if you are more senior and visible) are the request to review someone else's work. It is part of the duty of every researcher to review others' work in as timely and constructive a way as we would hope others would review ours. The whole system of peer-review works on goodwill, and I do not want to undermine that.

However, I think we sometimes feel a false sense of duty to review more than we need to. In the most extreme case I have heard, one researcher reviewed over 100 papers in a single year, explaining that the journal editors couldn't find anyone else and so kept coming back to him. In the end, he was accused of malpractice for suggesting that authors did more reading, which some authors perceived as a demand to cite the work he pointed them to. I'm not going to comment on this specific case, which also included his practice later on as a journal editor, as there has been no public scrutiny of the claims against this researcher or his defence. However, the bitterness of his open letters to the research community was palpable, given the time he had invested in the review process.

Reviewing is a thankless task, but we have to do it. The key point is to take a proportionate approach. Although it may be admirable to review over 100 manuscripts per year, I personally am not able to devote that amount of time to reviewing, if I want to achieve my most important goals and retain work-life balance. The question for me, therefore, is how many reviews should I do? There is no single right answer to this, but rather than accepting or declining every request, it is important to develop a rule of thumb that you feel is justifiable, so that you can do enough and then say "no" to any more with a clean conscience.

I personally feel that I have met my moral obligation to the research community if I review around three times as many manuscripts and grant proposals as I submit myself (on the basis that most of the papers and grants I submit will get three reviews each). In addition to only reviewing papers that are in my subject area, I will only review papers from which I think I'm likely to learn something useful or new (based on the abstract). This applies as much to abstracts claiming incremental advances on specific issues that I have researched as it does to manuscripts targeting the most prestigious journals. For grant reviews, I will tend to prioritise invitations to sit on funding panels, which usually requires multiple reviews, as I can learn more from this process about how to write a fundable proposal than I could by reviewing single proposals as part of a "peer-review college" (though I will review the odd proposal between panel invitations that is closely aligned to my research interests). I am not trying to suggest that this should be a generalisable rule of thumb that others should adopt; rather this is how I have rationalised what I feel is proportionate. Decide what you feel is proportionate, so you can say "no" to anything beyond this limit, without feeling bad about it.

How many meetings are enough?

Some organisations are worse than others when it comes to a culture of meetings, apparently for the sake of having meetings. In proportion, meetings are clearly a good way of communicating with colleagues, and moving forward together in collective endeavours. If you are spending a disproportionate amount of time in meetings, however, you may need to take stock and evaluate how necessary they are.

If you have called the meeting, then there is more you can do about it. The first question to ask yourself is whether or not the meeting is absolutely essential. If it is just an opportunity for people to update each other on progress, then might there be a more efficient way of doing that update and letting people actually get on with the work instead of spending an hour updating each other face-to-face. If in response to this question you realise that the update could be done more efficiently another way, but the real reason is to build a team and a culture, then ask yourself whether boring everyone in a meeting is the best way to achieve that goal, and perhaps have a team day out or invite everyone to lunch instead.

Many of the meetings we have to attend are called by senior colleagues, and we are mandated to attend. In my current role, every month I am expected to attend monthly a School Research Committee, a Centre management meeting, and chair a full day meeting and training of Knowledge Exchange Fellows. Bi-monthly, I chair an impact working group, attend another Centre management meeting, and chair an impact evaluation group and training programme for one of my projects. Less frequently, I contribute to regular advisory groups within and outside the university. On top of this, I have regular meetings for all the rest of the research projects I lead or contribute to. You can probably come up with similar lists.

Do you have to attend all of the meetings you are told you have to be at? If you do, do you have to be there every time? If there is nothing on the agenda you have to speak about or comment on, then would it matter if you missed the odd meeting, citing prior engagements (e.g. you have an urgent writing deadline – whether that deadline is self-imposed or externally imposed is not relevant to your colleagues). What would actually happen? Would the meeting cease to function? If you missed out on a key piece of information or decision, would there be no other way to find this out or influence that decision? Obviously, it is wise to check the agenda and if you're chairing the meeting, or have a key role you need to report on, then this won't be possible. Alternatively, is there someone you can share meeting duties with, taking it in turns to attend a regular meeting and reporting back briefly to each other, halving the number of meetings you each have to attend?

What do you do when you get stuck in a meeting that is going around in circles and clearly wasting your time? There are two things I regularly do that help me survive meetings like this. The first is to point out when you have reached the halfway point, explaining that you will have to leave at the end of the allotted meeting time. In as polite a way as possible, you are making it clear that extending the meeting indefinitely is not an option for the weak chair, and with luck, the chair will realise that they need to start steering the meeting more strongly to get through the agenda before time runs out. Sadly, this relies on the chair possessing the skill to manage the meeting more effectively, which may not be a valid assumption.

My second, and last resort, option therefore, is to subtly take the chair position myself. In a recent example, I handed back to a slightly stunned chair to close the meeting, and he told me after how grateful he was for my help. The reason he had been struggling to manage the meeting was because he had to contend with one particularly verbose colleague who was strongly disliked by another colleague whose frustrated body language gave way to some fairly offensive comments, taking the meeting off topic and into challenging territory. I conducted my subtle meeting takeover by suggesting that it was worth pausing to reflect on the key points and progress we had made so far (which was very limited), and that it might help if I did this on the whiteboard, so we could all keep track of where we were going (it was clear to most of us that we were currently going around in circles). As I stood to write on the whiteboard, everyone's eyes were on me, and my pen, and the act of standing with a pen in my hand was a powerful cue suggesting that I had the power to bring order and progress to the discussion. As we quickly started to make progress, the group gave its tacit approval for me to lead them.

Sometimes, however, feeling that their power is being undermined, a weak chair will react badly to an attempt by anyone else to get the meeting back on track. I was once at a workshop with over 100 stakeholders, which was being chaired by a very senior academic. The discussion was dominated by a few powerful individuals all morning, and by the morning break, people were complaining and making plans to leave early. I asked the chair if they had a professional facilitator I could talk to about how the meeting was going, and was informed that they were the facilitator, and that they would not be changing the style of the meeting. Things got worse after the break and a couple of people left, so I took things into my own hands and went round everyone in the room giving them all two Post-its™ each, slowly working my way to the front. When I reached the front, I suggested that everyone write their two best ideas on Post-its™ and we would cluster these on the wall, so we could build on everyone's ideas. I was told very clearly to sit down. Ouch.

Although not as universal as email and meetings, the digital realm is an increasing distraction for many researchers, and the next chapter will show you how you can take a new approach to your digital footprint that could actually save you time in your working day.

Key lessons

1. The tyranny of email lies not in the volume of emails we receive, but in how we perceive them. The only way to break this tyranny is to understand the negative feelings it gives voice to

2. Don't allow email to take you away from your prime focus. Focus on the things that are most important to you every day, so you can immediately recognise when tasks from your email are going to compromise the important goals you have said "yes" to

3. If you can't say "no", consider sending a holding email and replying later, putting the task on your to-do list so you can remain focused on your priorities now, or setting an "out of office" reply on writing days

4. Develop a "rule of thumb" to help you know when you can say "no" to reviewing other people's work, knowing that you are pulling your weight as a member of the research community

5. Give your apologies for all but the most essential meetings or take it in turns with a colleague to attend regular meetings, halving the number of meetings

Chapter 11
How to spend less time online

I am starting this chapter with the assumption that you have a digital footprint. By "digital footprint" I mean what someone sees when they put your name (or your name and employer if you have a common name) into an Internet search engine. Most researchers have an international profile, which is reflected in a level of visibility online.

You may be more or less happy with what you see, in terms of how up-to-date, professional and relevant it is, and you may feel that you get more or less back from the time you invest in managing your digital footprint. Some people spend many hours per week managing social media but would regard that as time well spent, based on the professional rewards it brings them (e.g. new collaborators, crowd-sourced answers to questions, discovery of grants they can apply for etc.). Others spend very limited time, just keeping their institutional profile up-to-date, but are happy with the visibility and opportunities it brings them. If you want to work out how much time you ought to be spending on digital platforms, you need to answer four questions.

1. Why am I online?

First, ask why you have a digital footprint. The answer might simply be that your employer demands that you have a profile on their website. If that is the only reason, and you have an institutional profile, then you have achieved your goal and need look no further.

Most researchers, however, have a wider range of reasons why they invest time online, for example, maintaining or extending professional networks, engaging with conference participants, whether they are at the conference in person or not, during and after the event, finding out about new research or funding opportunities before others, learning how stakeholder communities are discussing research topics and being prepared for their arguments, or actively driving specific beneficial impacts from research through a social media strategy that targets particular groups who are likely to benefit from the research in specific ways.

If you understand why you are online, you will be able to identify the extent to which your time online contributes towards or detracts from your most important goals, and adjust the amount of time you spend accordingly. If you think that online platforms will be an important way of achieving specific goals, then it is worth coming up with a strategy: specific actions you are taking online that help you reach specific goals. This could be an overarching digital strategy in which you clearly choose the platforms on which you place publications, or it could be a specific social media strategy.

Having a "strategy" doesn't mean you have to have anything written down. If you can answer the four questions in Box 5, you've already got a social media strategy. Now you just have to implement it to stop wasting time online and start driving benefits.

Box 5: Four questions to stop wasting time and start driving impact on social media

Are you wasting time on social media or is it helping you achieve impact? The easiest way to make sure your time on social media really counts is to have a social media strategy. If you can answer these four questions, then you've got yourself a social media strategy. Simple.

You don't have to write anything down – you just need to act on the answers to these questions to stop wasting time and start generating impacts on social media. Of course, if you want to write stuff down, this template is for you. Use the template below and the prompts on the following pages to pin down a clear strategy.

- What offline impacts do you want to achieve via social media?

- Who are you trying to reach, what are they interested in and what platforms are they on?

- How can you make your content actionable, shareable and rewarding for those who interact with you, so you can start building relationships and move the conversation from social media to real life?

- Who can you work with to make your use of social media more efficient and effective?

Download the full template with questions to help prompt more useful answers to the four questions above at: www.fasttrackimpact.com/resources

2. How much time do I spend managing my digital footprint?

Most people are not able to answer this question, and that is a problem because we may be spending significantly more time than we are consciously aware of. Although it may add up over time, most of us don't have a problem with the amount of time it takes to keep our various online profiles up-to-date. If this is a problem, consider rationalising the number of different profiles you have, shutting down profiles on services that don't give you many benefits for the time it would take to keep them up-to-date. If you're not able to get rid of some, consider how you might focus your attention on one or a few and link them together, sign-posting from one site to the others you want people to see first, to try and manage your profile more proactively.

Social media is more dangerous when it comes to time inputs. One of the reasons for this is that social media tends to blur the boundaries between personal and professional interests, so it is hard to know when professional activity has ended and you are simply pursuing personal interests. I like to regularly audit my social activity to find out how long I am spending (based on a time tracker app, over the last few years it has varied from 20-50 minutes, and is currently averaging around 35 minutes per day across three social networks that I use primarily for work). If you are not currently using social media, then there is a good possibility that one of the key reasons for avoiding it is the amount of time it would take. Many researchers have asked me how they can be expected to monitor multiple social media feeds when they can't even keep up with their emails. Saving time is just one of many very good reasons why many researchers avoid social media. However, if that is the only reason, and you think you might be able to benefit professionally from social media, then you might want to try the experiment I proposed in The Research Impact Handbook (replicated in Box 6 below).

3. Is my current digital strategy getting me what I want, and am I getting enough in return for the time I put in?

Whether you are using social media or not, it is important to take stock of the benefits you are deriving from the time you invest in managing your digital footprint. Some of the benefits are hard to measure, such as the visibility of your publications, but many platforms show you the number of views your publications are getting, which you might assume will eventually translate into citations. Other benefits may be more tangible, such as the answer to an important question or finding a new collaborator. The problem is that it is usually possible to point to some sort of benefit as a way of justifying the time we put in. Ask yourself if you genuinely feel that the benefits are worth it, for the time you are putting in, and if that time might be better spent on tasks that more directly contribute to your most important goals.

In addition to the benefits you get from social media, consider the problems it brings you as well. I've mentioned the problem of time already, but it is worth recognising the reputational dangers of social media. We have all heard of people in the news who have lost their jobs over a misjudged social media post. A tweet is not worth your job. If you have any niggling sense of doubt that what you are about to say could be taken out of context and used against you, or might not be entirely appropriate, don't say it. Save a draft, sleep on it, take advice from others, but don't risk your reputation for a tweet.

I once got into an online spat with a fan of *The Guardian* journalist George Monbiot. I was taking issue with some of the evidence underpinning his latest book, and nothing I said seemed to be getting through. Eventually, in my frustration, I said how much I used to respect his climate change journalism in the 1990s but that he had lost my respect now. Of course, George Monbiot himself was following this exchange, and he wasn't best pleased. I instantly apologised. What I had said was disrespectful and out of character. It might not have lost me my job, but I didn't feel proud of what I'd said. At that point, everyone else who had been following started to pitch in, saying that the discussion had just started to get interesting. One of these people was in charge of the Hay Festival, and invited us to debate the issues on stage. Clearly there was only one answer I could give, but if you have seen George debate you will understand why I instantly started researching courses on debating skills. The debate never took place in the end, which I was relieved about, but the strange thing is that I would probably have felt comfortable saying far more controversial things on stage, face-to-face, than I felt I had risked on Twitter.

Box 6: How to use social media and save time in your working day

Would you believe me if I told you that I actually save time by engaging with social media – about an hour of extra time in my working day to be precise?

What would you do with an hour of extra time per day? Most days I actually use the extra time to rest or indulge non-work interests and get better work-life balance. However, on busy days that hour can make the difference between having time to respond to my urgent emails or not, or it might give me time to accept an invitation to write a blog post and create something that gets my research to a wider audience.

To explain how, let me invite you to do an experiment with me…

1. **Work out how long you spend engaging with the news on an average day.** When I first did this, I listened to BBC Radio 4 Today for 10–30 minutes, the Six O'Clock News for 20–30 minutes, read news from the Yahoo or BBC News apps for 5–15 minutes, got news from Twitter for 5–15 minutes and spent between 30–50 minutes a week listening to the BBC World Service, reading *The National*, *The Guardian* and other newspapers. On average this added up to around 90 minutes per day.

2. **Replace your usual news with your own tailored news stream via Twitter.** Follow the radio and TV news programmes, apps and newspapers you currently use on Twitter. Given that most of these will offer their content free on the platform, you may want to consider donating to news organisations who allow this. Now find a few more specific news feeds that are relevant to your research, for example your professional body or society, your research funders and key researchers in your field. For one day this week, disengage from all other forms of news and only get your news from Twitter.

3. **See how much time you save.** I built my Twitter following (over 70,000 followers across my accounts) on about 20 minutes per day, but I now spend about 35 minutes per day, actively managing five accounts in different ways to achieve specific impact goals. My 35 minutes per day includes getting all my news, generating content and reaching out proactively to target groups. I now get more relevant news, tailored to my interests and am building my online influence and offline impacts, while giving myself 55 minutes per day of extra time.

4. Is there something more important I should be doing right now

Ask yourself this final question again and again, and keep coming back to it. You may have started by checking a message from a colleague that was posted to a particular digital platform, and gone on to look at the rest of the activity on your account, before noticing an interesting paper by someone in your network... Before you know it, an hour has passed. It may all be work-related and interesting, but it is only tangentially useful, and in reality it is delaying you from getting started on more important tasks. Very often there is something more important we should be doing, and online distractions are among the most alluring and self-deceptive forms of procrastination.

We all have a digital footprint, whether we like it or not. Some of us want to grow our digital footprint while others want it to shrink and go away. Whatever position you are in, the key point of this chapter is to show you how you can engage efficiently with your digital footprint, and not spend too much time on it. Much more could be said about gaining influence and becoming more productive online. I have included this chapter here because online activities are increasingly a source of distraction and can sap focus and motivation from researchers who could otherwise be far more productive. Improving the way you manage your digital footprint can help your overall productivity. The trick is to remain constantly vigilant of the risks that your digital footprint poses to your time and reputation.

Key lessons

1. If you want to work out how much time you ought to be spending on digital platforms, you need to know the following: what you want to achieve from the time you invest online; how much time you currently spend managing your digital footprint; how you are benefiting from the time you invest online; and whether there is something more important you should be doing instead.

2. Identify the reasons why you have a digital footprint and what benefits you want it to bring you. Turn this into a simple strategy that can help you focus your online activity to get maximum benefit from the time you invest

3. Audit your digital footprint and the amount of time you typically spend online. Be honest with yourself (or use a digital tracking tool to give you an honest answer). Start to be more aware of the time you are spending online, putting limits on this if necessary

4. Withdraw from platforms that don't give you enough benefits for the time you have to invest in them

5. Keeping asking yourself if you should be doing something more important, and remain aware of the risks of social media to your time and reputation at all times

Chapter 12
Conclusion

In this book, I have drawn on literature from psychology and organisational management to international development and ecology, interviews with some of the most productive researchers in the world, and my own personal experience. I have sought to draw out general principles and communicate them in ways that are immediately applicable.

Next steps

The next steps may not be easy. If you want to increase the chances of maintaining your new-found commitment to reaching your goals, you might want to get some backup. Social norms are powerful, and no matter how impervious we may perceive we are to the opinions of others, we become subtly influenced. Social learning theory suggests that all learning takes place in a social context and is mediated through our interaction with others. Even someone sitting alone, learning from a book, will interpret the words on the page within the cultural frame of reference they have been brought up in. We take advice from those we know and trust to inform or confirm the decisions we make. In the same way that a drug addict or alcoholic needs to get away from their old friends who still take drugs or drink if they want to stay clean, we need to surround ourselves with people who will help us make and stick to decisions that will enable us to reach our most important goals. Sometimes just one person can be the bridge to a whole new community of people who can help you achieve what you need.

Partly, this is about having access to a source of support and inspiration when achieving your goals requires sacrifice and you might otherwise give up. Partly, it is about accountability. By discussing your goals with someone important to you, in a way that articulates their deeper significance clearly, you are able to create a level of accountability that will give you greater staying power than you might otherwise have during wobbly moments. Some people tell the world via social media, some tell significant others, and some simply write their goals down.

Although the sample size was small (149 participants), research completed by Gail Mathews (Dominican University, California) in 2015 suggested that those who wrote down their goals and shared them with a friend were up to 33% more likely to say they had reached them or were at least halfway there after four weeks than those who did not write down their goals. Whether or not these precise figures are robust, they illustrate the idea that being accountable for your goals can increase the likelihood of reaching them.

Who can you discuss your goals with? Ask them if you can check in with them again after a few months, to see how things are progressing. Maybe you can do the same for them, and you can help each other become more accountable in the pursuit of your goals?

Personal reflection

This book started with a personal desire to understand how a small number of close colleagues and I were achieving higher than average levels of productivity. The answers to my questions took me, and hopefully you as well, to a much deeper than anticipated level of personal reflection.

My first experience as a researcher, in the mountain forests of Uganda, showed me the beauty and value of the research process. When we arrived, the forest was a tangled mess of green, but when we left I was able to read the history of that forest through the names of the species that grew there. In the same way, I hope that by studying your own motives, values and identity, you will have found goals that were always there; you just couldn't see them clearly before. There is a good chance that you won't feel comfortable with everything you found in that self-examination. Our Ugandan forest ranger told us the history that the trees bore witness to, as he took us to a patch of undergrowth and showed us the burned corner-posts of the house he had been born in. He proceeded to tell us how he had set it alight in his role as a park ranger, as part of a mass eviction, decades earlier.

Like that ranger and me, you may not feel very proud of some of the things you find in the undergrowth. However, I hope like me, you are also able to find new, more empowering narratives in the tangled branches and roots of the inner landscape you have explored while reading this book. These are narratives that accept and integrate your weaknesses and limitations as part of a broader conception of your strengths and overall character. I hope you now have goals that are Stretching, Motivational, Authentic, Relational and Tailored to these unique capabilities. These goals should not just be in your imagination, but you should now have a clearly structured plan to reach them, and based on Part 2 of this book, you should have some practical ideas about how you are going to put that plan into action.

Part of me hopes that, as a result, you will become significantly more productive. Another part of me hopes for something deeper: a new way of thinking about productivity, which is less about the work you produce and more about how you produce it. At the heart of this book is a type of productivity that is about producing a clearer conception of you. It is about seeing your unique, intrinsic value more clearly than ever before, and being able to express that in your work life, consciously, from moment to moment.

Remember why you first wanted to be a researcher. Remember your most inspiring achievement as a researcher. Remember who you are. When you remember why you are doing what you are doing, you will do it for the right reasons, and you will do it better. The fact that this enables you to cut out unnecessary tasks and become highly focused and productive is merely a by-product of reigniting your motivation and starting to seek your most important goals. The lessons in this book will make you more productive, but they will also make you more satisfied with what you produce, and I hope they will enable you to be happy working less, and being more.

Acknowledgements

Thanks to Frede Blaabjerg, Cornelia van Duijn, Gwojen Hwang and Kee Hung (Mike) Lai for taking the time to be interviewed for this book. Thanks to Ana Attlee, Chris Cvitanovic, Ioan Fazey, Jasper Kenter, Ian MacDonald, Rosmarie Neumann, Andrew Scott, Lindsay Stringer, Alister Scott, Hanifa Shah, Phil Ward and Dylan Young for insightful feedback and encouragement on the first draft of this book. Thanks to Dana MacGregor from the University of Durham for the "conversation in answer machine mode" analogy I used in Chapter 4. Chapter 10 builds on material from Chapter 10 of *The Research Impact Handbook*. The identity pie exercise and power questionnaire are based on exercises I was taught by Ben Fuchs.

Appendix 1: Ten of the most productive researchers in the world

Table A1: Data taken from Elsevier's SciVal tool, tracking research papers in the period 2011-15, published by Times Higher Education in December 2016. Each academic listed in the table has the highest average citation count across their papers in each broad subject area. The data include only researchers with many publications to their name in the period, so those who have garnered lots of citations with just a handful of papers have been filtered out.

Subject area	Name	Institution	Country	Research area
Computer science	Peng Shi	Victoria University	Australia	Computational intelligence
Biochemistry, genetics and molecular biology	Cornelia van Duijn	Erasmus University Rotterdam	Netherlands	Genetic epidemiology
Business, management and accounting	Kee Hung Lai	Hong Kong Polytechnic University	Hong Kong	Logistics and shipping
Chemistry	Michael Grätzel	École Polytechnique Fédérale de Lausanne	Switzerland	Photonics and interfaces
Economics, econometrics and finance	Daron Acemoglu	Massachusetts Institute of Technology	United States	Political economy
Engineering	Frede Blaabjerg	Aalborg University	Denmark	Energy and electronics
Mathematics	Francisco Herrera	University of Granada	Spain	Soft computing and intelligence information systems

Neuroscience	Ronald Karl Peterson	Mayo Clinic, Rochester	United States	Cognitive impairment and dementia
Physics and astronomy	Arnulf Quadt	University of Göttingen	Germany	Hadron collider physics
Social sciences	Gwojen Hwang	National Taiwan University of Science and Technology	Taiwan	Education and learning

Appendix 2: Power questionnaire

The following points, from The Research Impact Handbook (2016), are designed to help you identify the different types of power you possess in any given context. You can use this in a general sense (thinking about the main social group you belong to or interact with most), but it is most useful to think about how powerful you are in a specific context, for example, as a facilitator leading a workshop with people who are interested in your research. Imagine yourself in this situation, and rate how powerful you feel on a scale of 1–5 in relation to each of the following personal characteristics. You may do this in relation to how powerful you feel and/or how powerful you think the other people in this situation think you are (you will need to choose which of these you think most affects your ability to achieve impact).

Hierarchical power:
- Seniority in formal hierarchy
- Expertise
- Access to decision-makers

Social power:
- Race or ethnicity
- Age
- Gender
- Class or wealth
- Education level
- Strength and breadth of your social networks
- Title (e.g. Mrs, Dr or Prof)

Personal power:
- Self-awareness
- Self-confidence and assertiveness (not over-confidence)
- Charisma and strength of character
- Ability to empathise with others
- Life experience and ability to survive adversity
- Ability to communicate and influence others
- Reputation for integrity and honesty
- Creativity

- Honest estimation of your own worth and abilities, being aware of your limitations and weaknesses, whilst focusing on your strengths and abilities
- Being someone who believes in, trusts and builds others up, rather than criticising and gossiping

Transpersonal power:
- Connection to the other; to something larger, more significant and lasting
- Commitment to a positive and clear set of values and beliefs
- Being prepared to challenge the status quo rather than compromise your values
- Ability to overcome or forgive past hurts
- Freedom from fear
- Service to an altruistic vision or cause

Endnotes

[i] http://www.ucu.org.uk/media/6908/UCU-survey-of-work-related-stress-2014---summary-of-findings-Nov-14/pdf/ucu_stresssurvey14_ summary.pdf

[ii] https://www.ucu.org.uk/media/8196/Executive-summary---Workload -is-an-education-issue-UCU-workload-survey-report-2016/pdf/ucu_ workloadsurvey_summary_jun16.pdf

[iii] http://www.sigmaxi.org/docs/default-source/Programs-Documents/Critical-Issues-in-Science/postdoc-survey/highlights

[iv] https://www.aaup.org/issues/faculty-work-workload/what-do-faculty-do

[v] This was my understanding at the time. I clearly didn't understand the PhD I had applied for. I now work regularly with plant geneticists to generate social as well as economic benefits for farmers, communities and companies.

[vi] *Shifting Stories* – Andrew Scott (Matador, 2016) ISBN 9781785893551

[vii] Find out more at: www.sharedvaluesresearch.org

[viii] If you want to read more about these approaches, I've reviewed the behavior change literature in a couple of peer-reviewed articles which are available at www.sharedvalues.org